DOES GOD REALLY ANSWER OUR PRAYERS?

DOES GOD REALLY ANSWER OUR PRAYERS?

My Divine Appointment Story

JOHN CHRISTOPHER MYNYK

Foreword by Andrew Rappaport

RESOURCE *Publications* • Eugene, Oregon

DOES GOD REALLY ANSWER OUR PRAYERS?
My Divine Appointment Story

Resource Publications
An Imprint of Wipf and Stock Publishers
199 W. 8th Ave., Suite 3
Eugene, OR 97401

www.wipfandstock.com

PAPERBACK ISBN: 979-8-3852-4941-1
HARDCOVER ISBN: 979-8-3852-4942-8
EBOOK ISBN: 979-8-3852-4943-5
VERSION NUMBER 07/09/25

Some names and details have been changed to protect the privacy and anonymity of individuals involved. All else is true to the best of my recollection.

All Scripture quotations, unless otherwise indicated, are taken from the Holy Bible, King James Version.

To Jesus Christ, my Lord and Savior,
who schedules divine appointments with those he saves
and answers the prayers of his people.

Contents

Foreword | *xi*

Introduction | *xv*

Chapter 1   The Sermon | 1

Chapter 2   A Retired Minister's Plea | 3

Chapter 3   A Summer of Change | 5

Chapter 4   A Proper Approach to the Gospel | 7

Chapter 5   Majoring on the Minors | 14

Chapter 6   A Lost Opportunity | 17

Chapter 7   A Hire for Higher Education | 19

Chapter 8   A Master's in Confusion | 21

Chapter 9   The Passerby | 24

Chapter 10   The Curious Couple | 28

Chapter 11   The Plan | 31

Chapter 12   The Profession | 33

Chapter 13   The Enrollment | 36

Chapter 14   I'll Be Home Alone for Christmas | 40

Chapter 15   The Bible Club | 42

Chapter 16   Moving Off Campus | 45

Chapter 17   A Dissertation Proposed | 47

Chapter 18   A Dissertation Completed | 49

Chapter 19   An Oral Defense | 53

Chapter 20   A Failed Bible Lesson | 55

Chapter 21   A Conflict of Contracts | 57

Chapter 22   Ministering on Borrowed Time | 61

Chapter 23   Return of the Guests | 63

Chapter 24   A Storm Now and Then | 66

Chapter 25   A Second Chance | 68

Chapter 26   Search the Scriptures | 70

Chapter 27   A Friend's Approval | 72

Chapter 28   Saved by the Rain | 74

Chapter 29   Ishbibenob Slays the Crowd | 76

Chapter 30   A Life-Changing Dream | 78

Chapter 31   The Candy Man Can | 80

Chapter 32   The Day of Reckoning | 82

Chapter 33   It's Story Time | 85

Chapter 34   It's Time to Preach | 94

Chapter 35   The Quiz | 100

Chapter 36   The Confrontation | 102

Chapter 37   The Call to Nature | 105

Chapter 38   The Conversion | 106

Chapter 39   The Good News | 108

Chapter 40   A Hearty Congratulation | 111

Chapter 41   A Gift for the Convert | 112

Chapter 42   Patience Is a Virtue | 114

Chapter 43   Spinning Around in Circles | 116

Chapter 44   Third Time's a Charm | 119

Chapter 45   An End to a Contract | 122

Chapter 46   Goodbye Bible Club | 124

Chapter 47   Moving On | 127

Chapter 48   Reflections | 128

Chapter 39 The Good News | 108

Chapter 40 A Healthy Congratulation | 11[illegible]

Chapter 41 [illegible] | 112

Chapter 42 Fat[illegible] | 114

Chapter 43 [illegible] in Circles | 11[illegible]

Chapter 44 [illegible] | [illegible]

Chapter 45 A[illegible]

Chapter 46 [illegible]

Chapter 47 [illegible]

Chapter [illegible] Reflections [illegible]

Foreword

Let me start with a confession: I have never had a dramatic, lightning-bolt-from-heaven testimony. No burning bushes, no blinding lights on the road to Damascus, no sudden healings or voice-from-the-clouds moments. I was not delivered from a biker gang or rescued from a burning building while quoting Romans. Honestly, my story is pretty normal. And for years, I thought that made it less useful, less inspiring, even thought it was boring. I figured God reserved the cool stories for other people—you know, the ones who get invited to speak at conferences.

But then I picked up this book.

What you are about to read is not a tale of jaw-dropping miracles or headline-making answers to prayer. It is something much rarer and, in my opinion, much more relatable: a story of persistent faith, unglamorous trust, and down-to-earth, everyday prayer. It is about real life—and thank God for that.

This book is like a conversation over coffee with a friend who has been through it. It is honest, humble, and at times hilariously human. You will not find any spiritual theatrics or overproduced testimonies here. Instead, what you will find is encouragement for the rest of us—the ones who pray, and wait, and wonder if we are doing this whole Christian life right.

The author and I share a heart for evangelism. We want people to come to know Jesus. But let us be honest—sometimes we feel like we need a Hollywood-level story to really make an impact. Like we need explosions and plot twists for people to take the gospel seriously. And if we do not have that, we wonder if our testimony is even worth telling.

Enter this book. It reminds us that the power of the gospel is not in how flashy our story is, but in how faithful our God is. Spoiler alert: he is very faithful.

The beauty of this personal account lies in its simplicity. It is easy to read because it feels like real life. It is not trying to impress you—it is trying to walk with you. And that makes all the difference. The author does not preach at you; they invite you into their own questions, their own moments of waiting, and their own small (but deeply meaningful) encounters with God.

Let me tell you—there were times reading this where I thought, "Wait, did he just read my journal?" Because the emotions, the frustrations, the dry spells in prayer—they are all in here. And instead of pretending to have all the answers, the author shows us that sometimes just showing up in prayer is the victory.

And that is something we do not talk about enough in the church. We love the big testimonies—and rightly so! But most of us live in the in-between. We are not always on the mountaintop. Sometimes we are in the spiritual equivalent of a traffic jam, just trying to inch forward without losing our sanctification. This book speaks to that space.

It is like a warm blanket of reassurance that says, "Hey, it is OK if your story does not involve a burning bush. Keep praying. Keep trusting. God sees you."

One of my favorite parts about this book is how it celebrates small victories. We often want the Red Sea to part before we feel like God is moving. But what about the days we choose to trust him when nothing big is happening? What about the quiet moments when we decide to pray again, even though we did not get the answer we wanted last time? Those moments are sacred too.

There is also a lot of subtle humor in these pages—not slapstick comedy or stand-up routines, but the kind of chuckle-worthy observations that make you say, "Yep, been there." Like praying for patience and then getting stuck in the slowest checkout line known to mankind. Coincidence? I think not.

And through all the humor, the real-life struggles, and the heartfelt reflections, there is one constant message: God is listening. Even when you do not feel it. Even when your prayers seem to bounce off the ceiling. Even when the miracle doesn't come wrapped in the packaging you expected.

For those of us passionate about reaching the lost, this book is a timely reminder that evangelism is not about impressing people—it is about showing them who God is. And nothing shows the character of God quite like a believer who keeps praying, keeps loving, and keeps showing up even when the spotlight is off.

So, if you have ever felt like your story is not "good enough" for God to use—congratulations. You are exactly the kind of person he loves to work through. This book proves that. It is a field guide for the faithful. A devotional disguised as a memoir. A reminder that even the smallest prayers reach the ears of the Almighty.

Whether you are a seasoned prayer warrior or someone who forgets to pray until you are halfway through your morning coffee (no judgment), you will find encouragement here. You will find honesty, laughter, conviction, and maybe even a nudge to dust off your prayer journal.

And who knows? Maybe you will come away realizing that your "boring" testimony is not boring at all. Maybe you will see that every quiet moment of trust, every whispered prayer, every long season of waiting—is part of a bigger story. A story God is writing with care, precision, and more grace than we can imagine.

So, grab your favorite beverage, get comfy, and dive in. Let this book be the friend who reminds you that you are not alone, that your prayers matter, and that God is working—even in the silence.

Because honestly? That is the real miracle.

Striving to Make Today an Eternal Day for the Glory of God
Pastor Andrew R. Rappaport
Executive Director:
StrivingForEternity.org
ChristianPodcastCommunity.org
April 12, 2025

Introduction

"God answers prayers!" That's what they would tell me—"they" being Christian family, friends, and pastors. To people like me, it has always sounded superficial. Life would be good, normal, and natural. I'd live like there is a God, but not see evidence of it. Exactly what kinds of prayers get answered? How and when does he answer them? There doesn't seem to be a formula, but it seems like everyone else acts like there is.

I remember one Wednesday evening church service at Pensacola Christian College in the fall of 1999. A guest preacher spoke about how God answers prayers. In one of his stories, he was a college student who lacked the money to pay his tuition. He said that he prayed for the money. It came just in time the bill was due. An anonymous check covered the bill to the exact amount.

"Things like that just don't happen to a guy like me!" he said—his voice dropping to a quieter, humble tone. "God answers the prayers of *other* Christians—the mighty ones, but I'm different. I'm nothing special. I'm unworthy."

I'd hear those kinds of stories spewed from behind pulpits my whole life. I wouldn't know what to make of them other than that they mostly seem to apply to people in full-time ministry. Perhaps little prayers get answered in little ways for the average Christian like me? Big prayers get answered in big ways to full-time ministers?

I remember the following evening after that service. The men students in our four neighboring dormitory rooms gathered together for what the college would call "prayer group" as they would every Monday, Tuesday, Thursday, and Friday evening. After singing a couple of Christian choruses, we began mentioning prayer requests. Unless I wanted prayers for passing midterm or final exams, I had nothing to say.

"So, what did you all think of the sermon last night?" the prayer leader asked. "Has God ever answered any of your prayers specifically?"

I couldn't respond, neither could anyone else.

"I don't think God has ever answered any of my prayers like that either," he said. "I too need money to pay this month's tuition. I don't know what else I could do about it now but pray."

Fortunately, I didn't have that problem. Sure, money was tight. I had to work outside in the hot Florida sun to pay what I could of my tuition—about 75 percent, but Mom would come through with the remaining expenses. Perhaps I was unworthy of any miraculous answers to prayers because my needs were already met with natural circumstances.

About two weeks later, as we met for "prayer group," we began discussing prayer requests as usual. After the prayer requests mentioned by the group, it was time for the prayer leader to put in his two cents.

"So, guys, do you remember that sermon from over two weeks ago about the pastor who had his prayer answered specifically to the dollar amount?" he said. "Well, the same thing just happened to me. This morning, I saw an anonymous check in my mailbox. It was the exact amount I needed to the dollar to cover my bill."

"Praise the Lord!" a peer erupted. We were all stoked about the good news.

"I guess God does answer prayers," the prayer leader said. "He did promise to supply all of our needs."

Of course God was supplying all of our needs. He supplied the remainder of my tuition from my mom. He supplied my friend's tuition through an anonymous check. Could the anonymous check be a strange coincidence? Could it have simply been from a friend or relative that heard about his need and decided to act upon it? Regardless, all of us had our needs supplied.

However, I did have a prayer that I wanted answered—one I had made two years ago. A guest preacher at our home church talked about something called "divine appointments" that he had described as divinely guided opportunities to share the gospel with people that resulted in their salvation. I had asked God to give me one of these "divine appointments," but had yet to see anything like this transpire.

If I was going to have a "divine appointment" with someone, it had to be amazing. It had to seem like a supernatural coincidence. It had to seem more amazing than any of the ones that guest preacher had mentioned. It had to blow my mind.

Who was I kidding? I wasn't a pastor or a missionary. All of my attempts to share the gospel with someone were in vain. What if God actually answers prayers like that from Christians who aren't pastors or missionaries? What if I just needed patience? What if this "divine appointment" was with someone who hadn't even been born yet?

I've heard the mantras about how God answers prayers. I can't number the times I've heard a preacher say, "Jesus said in Matt 21:22: 'And all things, whatsoever ye shall ask in prayer, believing, ye shall receive!'" It sounds too easy, but then I've heard other preachers say, "Jas 4:3 says, 'Ye ask, and receive not, because ye ask amiss, that ye may consume it upon your lusts.'" What are we to make of all the madness? Does God really answer our prayers or not? Do we really know if our prayers are being rejected because we're "asking amiss?"

Talk can be cheap and mantras can be idle words. If you're like me, you may need more than clichés or quotations from Scripture to convince you that there really is a God out there who does care about us. If you are experiencing any doubts or discouragement in this crazy world and need to hear a true story that will restore your faith in God, perhaps my story will blow your mind about the amazing God we serve.

CHAPTER 1

The Sermon

There he stood behind the pulpit—another typical guest speaker. Yes, I'd seen him before—not him, but his kind—gray hair and a Texan twang—nothing unique for a Wednesday evening at our old country church in northeastern Pennsylvania. It was the fall of 1997. At seventeen, I was old enough to know that there's nothing new under the sun.

"Let me tell you . . . about divine appointments." His words caught me off guard. What are divine appointments? My eyes glued to him. I had to hear more.

Story after story surged from the pulpit—stories of the winding paths that brought people into the preacher's company. I remember one being about a flat tire that brought a woman to the mechanic the preacher was visiting.

". . . and now I'm here talking to you," the lady in his story concluded.

"You have a divine appointment with the Lord." That was the preacher's response to her before explaining how he led her to faith in the gospel of Jesus Christ.

Guest speakers had graced our pulpit with stories of evangelism before, but never in this manner. This wasn't an eccentric excuse to step on our toes and tell us to evangelize more. This was the testimony of a humble, kindly old man privileged to share what God had done in his life.

"Divine appointments," he concluded, "will you see them when they come . . . and, when they come . . . will you be ready to take them on?"

I lay in bed that night, captivated by the guest speaker's words. Were so-called "divine appointments" a real thing? Were they even biblical or were they something he made up?

A story from Acts 8 came to mind. It's about an Ethiopian eunuch who was reading Isa 53:7 and trying to understand it. The Holy Spirit moved a man named Philip to visit him. Philip explained that the passage was about Jesus, causing the Ethiopian to believe the gospel. After Philip baptized the eunuch, the Holy Spirit caught Philip away.

That story at least *sounded* like a "divine appointment" from the Bible. Wanting to believe the guest speaker's discourse, I looked toward the ceiling and prayed.

"God, if 'divine appointments' are real, could you give me one of these?"

Assuming my words to be meaningless drivel, I rolled over and slipped into dreamland.

CHAPTER 2

A Retired Minister's Plea

It was another Saturday morning—a time to enjoy a hearty brunch to perk us up for another day in the computer lab. My twin brother Daniel and I were second-semester computer science majors at Pensacola Christian College (PCC) in Florida—two years after I had heard the "divine appointments" sermon. Our C programming assignments were calling our names, but so were the generous helpings of bacon, sausage, and hash browns sizzling on the griddle in the cafeteria.

"Hey, guys. We're planning to do some door-to-door this morning. Wanna come?"

Alas! Someone was vying for our attention! Three young men stood near the lobby door of the dormitory, beckoning us; they wanted fresh meat to join them on their Christian crusade and bacon wasn't on the menu. Looks like they got to us before the hash browns did. Putting our convictions before our cravings, we turned away from the door to confront the three Musketeers.

"Sure. We'll join you," we said.

Fifteen minutes later with no more recruits, the Furious Five marched onward to battle. Perhaps, without an extra car, it was just as well no more had joined. As sardines in a small sedan can, we made our way downtown—parking near an apartment complex.

3

"I'll take Daniel and John with me," our fearless leader said, saluting his comrades. "You two go left and we'll go right."

The three of us marched down the sidewalk, ready to slay unsuspecting apartment dwellers with the Sword of the Spirit.

"You woke me up!" *slam*

"I have laundry to do!" *slam*

"I'm not interested in spiritual things!" *slam*

We got the typical, understandable responses; people just wanted to survive Saturday morning. They didn't want to be interrupted by strange men holding Bibles. Fortunately for us, our last encounter broke the monotony.

Knock, knock—an elderly man answered his door.

"Hello, I'm John," I greeted, "and this is my brother and our friend."

I gave him the usual spiel—we're just there to share with him the good news of Jesus Christ, asking him if he knows he's going to heaven.

"Shhh," the man replied. "Yes I do."

Why did he shush us? My curiosity grew.

Glancing around like he was James Bond hiding from Soviet assassins, the man gave us a wink. He then proceeded to explain his secret identity—a retired minister who just wanted to get along with his neighbors. He had no desire to scare them away with any religious discussions.

"I'm cool with you guys talking to my neighbors," he said, "but just don't get carried away."

Having informed him that we had already talked to them, he winked back nervously. After reminding us once again not to scare his neighbors away, he wished us a farewell.

"Well, that was odd," I mumbled to our leader as we walked back to the car.

"I know." He laughed. "As a retired minister, he should've been glad we're doing for his neighbors what he's not willing to do."

CHAPTER 3

A Summer of Change

I t was late spring of 2000—Daniel's and my sophomore year was coming to a close. As we were preparing for another grueling minimum-wage summer job in Pennsylvania, the PCC administration made a special announcement for computer science majors—a job opportunity on the college campus. No, it wasn't for fixing Y2K bugs. It was an opportunity to engineer the homeschooling curriculum for the Internet. Many would apply, but few would be chosen.

After most applicants were weeded out for a handful of the brightest minds, Daniel was chosen, but I was left out of the picture. Nearing twenty years old, our dreams of ditching grueling summer jobs for minimum wage were coming true, at least for one of us.

I couldn't be more proud of Daniel. Christians from all around the world would get to access the famous homeschooling curriculum from the comfort of their home computers, all thanks to his brilliance. What an opportunity after having been a student for only two years! He'd enjoy an air conditioned office, a $7.50-an-hour wage, free room and board, and no need for a car to commute. Who could have asked for a better way to begin the summer?

Up to this point, Daniel and I had always stuck together. We shared the same room, the same summer jobs, the same car, and the same computer, but now we'd be separating for a whole *summer*? I had to make a decision. If I were to move to Pennsylvania that summer, I'd be waking up early, working for only six dollars an hour, and spending money on long commutes. On the other hand, if I stayed at the college, I'd at least enjoy the same wages and free room and board as Daniel. The choice was clear; I was staying. I just had to apply for a summer work contract and accept whatever job the employment office would grant.

Apparently, my experience stacking boxes of veal cutlets and slipping CD's into sleeves from my past two summers wasn't relevant. However, my four semesters in the college's grounds department merited me the same for the summer. For the next four months, I'd be baking in the hot Florida sun while pulling weeds and mowing lawns. Daniel, on the other hand, would be learning valuable coding skills in a dignified and privileged opportunity.

Life didn't seem fair, yet it may not have been without its providence. Daniel had just earned an opportunity in the information technology (IT) department via his scholastic achievements. He'd soon have valuable connections. Certainly, if the IT department liked him (and I saw no reason they wouldn't), perhaps I'd soon join him in the ranks.

I was a late bloomer. If Daniel could get me into the IT department soon, I'd be forever grateful. If not, at least I could brag that he had earned his mark on the college. In the end, we both anticipated long careers in software development regardless of our opportunities as college students.

CHAPTER 4

A Proper Approach to the Gospel

That summer in grounds, I gained a new friend and work companion—Bryce. Bryce, a pastoral ministries major, outranked me two years by age, but lagged one year behind in college classification. Pulling weeds was our main responsibility together; we kept the flower beds clean both at the college and at the academy down the road. Of course, being the good pastoral ministries major that he was, Bryce soon wouldn't hesitate to ask me that important question:

"Would you like to do some door-to-door with me this Saturday morning?"

Why *wouldn't* he ask? Sharing the gospel is one of those things Christians are expected to do, right? After all, this is a *Christian college*. It was the summer—no excuses such as being bogged down with homework. I couldn't get out of this one. I reluctantly agreed. After expressing my concerns over my inexperience with this sort of thing, he assured me that he'd do most of the talking. I had nothing to lose.

That Saturday morning, I hopped into Bryce's car and rode to a neighborhood of small houses downtown. There I was, once again, surrounded by doors—doors ready to slam in my face. I was shaking, but my friend stood confident. At least I could keep him company while hiding in his shadow. I was now his student; he could show me the ways.

First, we'd like to go for what's behind door number one.

Knock, knock

"Yes?" a man answered. He was a burly jock in an A-shirt. An amber bottle hung from his hand.

"Hello, my name's Bryce and this is my friend John," my brave companion said. "We're just going around inviting people to church. Do you go to a church, sir?"

"No."

Bryce's eyes leapt onto the bottle. "I couldn't help but notice that beer in your hand. Don't you know that drinking is a sin?"

Perhaps Bryce was jumping to conclusions. For all we knew, that bottle could have been the man's key to self defense. What if we look at this from an outsider's shoes? If two young men come to one's home ready to talk about clouds, angels, demons, and fire, perhaps that bottle could be smashed over a countertop and used to deter them away. In all seriousness, that bottle was the man's choice of beverage.

"Look, man," the occupant growled. "I don't have time to stand here and listen to you preach. Have a good day."

Door number one got slammed in our faces. Perhaps we'd like to go for what's behind door number two?

"Well, that was rude." Bryce chuckled. "I guess he felt guilty of his sins and didn't wanna talk."

I stood there, pondering his words. Inviting people to church? Drinking is a sin?—not the kind of subjects I've ever heard in a gospel outreach. Perhaps it was a different tactic my veteran partner would prove to my skeptical mind?

Approaching the second door, my brave friend knocked once again. Out popped another burly man. With no bottle this time, the conversation could be fruitful. Alas! A lit cigarette rested between his fingers! I already knew where this was going.

"Hello, my name is Bryce and this is my friend John. We're just going around inviting people to church. Do you go to a church, sir?"

"Yes, I do," the man said.

"Well, that's good to know."

Bryce's eyes turned to the steaming stick in the man's hand. Here we go again!

"I couldn't help but notice that you've got a cigarette there. Did you know that smoking is a sin?"

"No, I didn't," the man snapped.

"Well, not only is it a sin, but it's bad for your health. I'd recommend you stop smoking as soon as possible. Do you think God will use you with a cigarette in your hand?"

"That's none of your business, sir! I love God and I go to church. Have a good day." The stranger slammed his door.

"Man, these people just don't wanna listen to reason." Bryce laughed. "The devil's blinding them from the truth."

Perhaps my experienced friend was getting warmed up. Surely the person in house number three would fall to his knees and believe the gospel, right? What if, instead, house number three held a drug cartel? That certainly would earn a cherry on top of our "successful dialogues!" Just in case, I had to ask my friend to clarify his tactics.

"Are you sure we should talk to people like that?" I asked.

"Like what?"

"I don't understand how talking about church, smoking, and drinking leads to the gospel."

"Because sin's what keeps people away from Christ." Bryce shook his head and smiled. "What would *you* suggest?"

"Well, I usually begin with: 'We're sharing the good news about Jesus. Do you know if you're going to heaven?'"

I figured Bryce would understand, but he scowled as if I were in my own world.

"People don't like to have the gospel shoved down their throats," he said. "It scares them away. It's better to begin a conversation and then ease your way into it."

I stood there, unable to conjure a response.

"Look," Bryce said, "if you're really certain your approach is better, why don't you prove it? Go ahead and take the next house."

Had I just planted my foot in my mouth? I was now expected to *prove* myself? Talk is cheap. Would I be able to add merit to my approach?

Marching to a small house not much bigger than a trailer, I gave the door a quick knock. I stood shaking for half a minute, but no one answered. I was ready to apologize to Bryce and let him take back the reins, but, suddenly, the knob began to jiggle.

Creaking open slowly, the door revealed a frail old man peeking cautiously through the crack; the look on his face portrayed someone who hadn't received many visitors. Fortunately for him, nothing controversial was in his hands.

After greeting the old-timer with my typical explanation of why we were there, I glanced back at Bryce for approval. He smiled, holding out his hand for me to continue.

"Do you know for sure that you're going to heaven?" I said.

Opening the door, the man hunched down, glaring into my eyes. He scowled and thought for a moment.

"How can you know for *sure*?"

My eyes rushed back to Bryce who was already rolling his at me. My heart began to race. *Could this be the "divine appointment" I had prayed for?* What should I say next? I didn't know much Scripture at the time—not even the Romans Road.

"Here, let me show you." I cleared my throat, forcing myself to continue. I turned to John 3:16.

"The Bible says, 'For God so loved the world, that he gave his only begotten Son, that whosoever believeth in him should not perish, but have everlasting life.' God sent Jesus to die on the cross to pay for our sins. All we have to do is believe that and we can know for sure we're going to heaven."

Smiling back, the old man pointed his bony finger at me and quoted John 6:37: "'All that the Father giveth me shall come to me; and him that cometh to me I will in no wise cast out.'"

"Amen," I said. "So, do you know for sure you're going to heaven?"

"I hope so."

"But it's not a matter of hope!" I preached. "It's a matter of faith! You just said that everyone that comes to him he will not cast out. I just showed you that anyone who believes in Jesus will have everlasting life. Do you believe in Jesus as your personal Lord and Savior?"

"Yes, I do." The man smiled back. "I asked Jesus to save me when I was a child."

I pressed the man further, explaining that true faith in the gospel is not merely a matter of hope, but a matter of faith in Jesus. The man concluded that if God will not cast out anyone who comes to him in faith that it must mean that he's certain that he's saved. I rejoiced with him in his claim to faith in Jesus.

"Well, I need to go check on my laundry," he said. "Thank you so much for talking to me about Jesus. I really appreciate it."

As the kindly old man shut the door, I turned to Bryce. He looked as if he were thinking.

"Well, that was kind of fun," I said with a laugh. "I'm not sure if I actually accomplished anything. Maybe the man was already saved. I don't know what to make of that."

"Yeah, well, you did your best," Bryce said, "and that was a really good conversation. Maybe you proved me wrong. Go ahead and try the next house."

My nerves began to dwindle as I marched up to the next door and knocked. Having given the same introduction, I assumed it would yield a similar response.

"Sorry, not interested. Have a good day," the occupant said, slamming his door.

The next three encounters were no different.

"John, I know you mean well," Bryce said, "but I just don't think your approach is working. I told you people don't want the gospel shoved down their throats."

Dejected, I gave him the lead once again. Unfortunately, the rest of our conversations yielded similar responses.

At the end of our patrol, we found ourselves in a backyard barbecue. Several men reclined on lounge chairs, one man operated the grill, and a gray-haired man smoked a cigarette near the house.

"Hello," Bryce said. He greeted with a wave.

"Hello," a reclining man greeted back. "What brings you fellows here?"

"I'm Bryce and this is my friend John. We're just going around inviting people to church. Do you currently attend a church?"

"Yes, I do."

Bryce's eyes locked onto the questionable items. "I couldn't help but notice that you're drinking beer and your friend is smoking a cigarette. Smoking and drinking are bad for you. If you really want God to use you, I'd suggest you quit smoking and drinking as soon as possible."

The man in the chair pondered for a moment. "I'm sure God's OK with it. I mean I pray to him a lot."

"Well, do you really think God would answer your prayers when you have that beer in your hands?" Bryce said.

The man looked nervous—unable to answer. His gray-haired friend by the house marched to his rescue, chuckling like he was ready to take us to school.

"Here, let me handle these guys for you." The old man laughed through an unnaturally raspy voice. "Looky here. That man's my son. We all just wanna enjoy a nice cookout and you think you can come here and tell us what we *can* and *can't* do in front of God? That's *his* business, not *yours!*"

"Sorry, sir," said Bryce. "We apologize."

"It's OK." The old man chuckled. "I just wanna tell you something. About a year ago, I was diagnosed with throat cancer."

"Oh, my. I'm sorry to hear that."

"No need to apologize. I'm completely fine with it. Every day I wake up and the first thing I do is pray to God and thank him that I'm still alive."

"Really? Good for you."

"Yes. I've learned to appreciate every single day. Sure, I still smoke and drink occasionally and I even talk to God about it. I have a lot of personal time alone with him—just me and God. I just thank him every day that I'm still alive."

"That's good!" Bryce cheered.

"I just want you to know that we're people who believe in God," the elder lectured. "Our smoking and drinking is our own business, not yours. I'd encourage you not to go around criticizing people for doing stuff that's really none of your business."

"OK, sir," said Bryce. "We'll take that into consideration."

On that note, our morning evangelism opportunity came to an end. Bryce and I returned to the car.

"Man, I feel sorry for those people," said Bryce, "especially that old man. He's obviously killing himself with that cigarette and he refuses to quit."

"Yeah, I know," I said. "Too bad we didn't get a chance to share the gospel with them."

"They wouldn't have listened anyways. They all claimed to have a personal relationship with God. There's nothing we could have told them to change their minds."

"I agree. But I just wish that we could've talked about something else besides church, beer, and cigarettes."

"People's sins keep them from Jesus," he said. "Unless they're willing to give up their sins they won't accept the gospel."

I didn't know what to think that day. I still assumed that my approach was the better one, yet neither approach garnered a fruitful conversation, save the one I had with the kind old man. Bryce's approach assumed that sin prevented people from accepting the gospel, which is technically true. My approach assumed that the good news of Jesus Christ is what would save people from their sins, which is also technically true. I assumed that people would first need to hear good news that would eventually give them a reason to give up any sins, but what did I know? I was just a young computer science student. Was there even such a thing as a correct approach to the gospel?

CHAPTER 5

Majoring on the Minors

I t was mere weeks until the summer of 2001 and the Internet project was far from complete. Like a year ago, a professor in a chapel service asked computer science students to apply for the summer opportunity. Alas, only three loyalists answered the call—Daniel was one of them. The IT department still needed one more to fill the team, but no one else responded.

Perhaps applicants from the previous year now had other opportunities or internships. Perhaps a half-finished project wasn't as appealing as a new project. Perhaps the professor couldn't make the project sound as exciting as it was last year. Whatever the reason, Daniel seized the opportunity for Yours Truly.

"Well, you know, my twin brother John is here," Daniel said to the IT manager. "He'd love to help out."

"I know that," said the manager, "but I'm not sure about twins working together in the IT department."

"I understand, but, if you're running out of time and need more volunteers, he's here eager and capable for the job. . . . Just saying."

"OK. You've convinced me. Let him know that he's hired."

Since last summer, Daniel had been transferred from the print shop to the IT department. I, having put in a summer and six semesters of work into the grounds department, had been preparing my mind for another sweltering summer. That afternoon, Daniel came to my rescue with a surprise announcement. What are twin brothers for?

Of course, what was good news to me wasn't as much for my manager on grounds. He still gave me a hearty congratulation. I returned the favor with the best last two weeks I could of pulling weeds and mowing lawns. At this point, I figured that grounds would become a distant memory—being replaced by IT.

It was a summer of writing code and cracking jokes with Daniel, two students, and two computer science professors—the best summer I've ever had at PCC. As expected, Daniel and I continued working on the Internet project the following two semesters. Alas, graduation began lurking around the corner with the Internet project far from complete. We wanted to see it through. We just needed some excuse to stay.

A professor in chapel one morning solved our dilemma with a special announcement—a new e-business minor was entering the catalog. What in the world was e-business? My curiosity got the best of me.

The following afternoon, I rushed to the records office to snatch up an early print of the courses for the e-business minor. That evening, Daniel and I poured over the schedule. It contained basic art classes, graphic design classes, and web programming classes—everything to scratch the artistic itch on any computer programmer's body. We were mesmerized.

"Are we sure we want to graduate now?" I asked. "I really like this e-business minor."

Daniel nodded slightly. "I'd also like to finish the Internet project. It seems like we're the only students remaining who've worked on it."

"Is there a reason why we shouldn't stay an extra year?" I prodded. "We can finish both the Internet project and this e-business minor."

After an evening of debate and brainstorming, the decision was unanimous; we were staying an extra year to "major" in the new e-business minor and finish the Internet project.

CHAPTER 6

A Lost Opportunity

Merrily, merrily, merrily, merrily, life was but a dream that first semester in the e-business minor. We felt like giddy children in art class—drawing physical patterns on paper, designing logos and ads on computers, and programming beautiful websites. At work, I was casually coding a graphical interface for editing online homeschooling tests. College couldn't get more fun than this! What ever could go wrong?

One morning, as I sat at work coding away and whistling in ignorant bliss, our IT team leader approached; his face hung.

"John, I hate to tell you this," he said, "but the Internet project was unexpectedly cancelled yesterday afternoon."

"*How?*" I was shocked.

"The president called, asking how the project was going. At one point, he told me to answer this honestly: 'Are the tests online just as easy to take as if they were on paper?' When I told him 'No,' he said, 'Then cancel the project and let its programmers go.' There was nothing I could say or do about it."

My heart sank from my chest. The two summers and almost three semesters from me, along with the three summers and almost five semesters from Daniel had, just amounted to nothing.

"Does this mean that we're doing other IT work now?" I asked.

"Unfortunately, no," he said. "It means you're out of a job. You'd have to reapply for another work contract and accept wherever they place you. I'm very sorry about this."

"I understand," I assured the man. "This is no one's fault. It's just how things happen."

With less than half a semester remaining, Daniel and I found ourselves unemployed. We figured we wouldn't fret over the situation. We'd simply enjoy the rest of the semester then reapply for work the following. One more semester working somewhere else couldn't be that bad, right?

One evening, as I examined the catalog for the remaining e-business classes, some unknown details brought back another debate with Daniel. We had just discovered the class schedule's rigid structure. The e-business minor had to be spread over two years. If we really wanted to finish what we had started, we'd have to stay yet another year. With the Internet project off the table, we couldn't use it as an excuse.

"I feel odd about staying yet another year," I said, "but I really want to finish the e-business minor."

"I know," Daniel added. "I'd like to stay for next semester, but I really don't wanna stay for another year after that just for this minor. If you're really gonna finish the minor, I'll see if I can get a staff contract in IT after next semester. We can still be here together while we figure out our next steps."

"Sounds like a plan!"

CHAPTER 7

A Hire for Higher Education

The cancellation of the Internet project and the loss of our IT jobs had put a damper on the plans Daniel and I had, but it wasn't without its upsides. For Daniel's final semester and my final year as undergraduates, we were assigned jobs in the dining services department. My diligence at my job in housekeeping earned me five "extra effort awards." For my final summer contract, I worked in the distribution center in their picking line, breaking all picking records and being declared "best picker ever" by the manager.

These unexpected achievements were a joyful experience, but reality began setting in once again. Daniel had received his diploma after the spring semester and began a full-time staff position in the IT department starting that summer. I was working on completing the e-business minor for that final year. I was in the middle of the fall semester with only the remaining spring semester left to plan my next step in life.

"Are you a senior unsure of what you want to do next?" It was a speech professor during a chapel service one morning. She didn't realize she was talking directly to me. "Perhaps you're not at the top of your class and want to know how to set yourself apart from the crowd."

Was she reading my mind? That had to be impossible from at least five hundred feet away!

"One way to do that is to get a master's degree," she said.

Having lived at PCC for about five and a half years, I wasn't ignorant of the subject. However, no one had ever advertised graduate programs in chapel before. I was intrigued, but still reluctant.

"It doesn't even have to be in your field of study," she added. "A master's in a completely unrelated subject shows people that you're flexible and willing to learn."

Her words gripped me by the collar and wouldn't let go. Every other thought I had that day escaped me. She had me hooked; I had to get a master's degree.

After the professor's marketing pitch, at least three other professors pitched their subjects of expertise: history, education, and fine arts. None of those subjects interested me, but the pitches pulled me in. They explained how their skills could impress potential employers in interviews. I knew what I had to do as soon as possible—go master's degree shopping.

At my next free hour, I visited the information desk to inquire about master's degrees. Frantically poring over the list of available programs, I found nothing of interest except one—art. Before gathering any sense of logic, I found myself scheduling an appointment with the dean of art the following week. I'd have to explain to him why he should allow me to enroll in the Master of Art program. Was I even ready for such a pitch?

CHAPTER 8

A Master's in Confusion

There I sat in an unfamiliar office. It wasn't the most elaborate office, but it was clean—cozy. My heart pounded. I needed the right words. I was going to enroll in a master's program. Finally, I was ready to become somebody!

The door creaked open. There stood the man ready to change my life—hair neatly combed and parted. His dark suit and tie demanded respect. He sat behind the desk—leather briefcase clapped onto the surface. Clearing his throat and adjusting his tie, he smiled slightly.

"What can I do for you?"

"I'd . . . like to enroll in the Master of Art program?" I said, grinning sheepishly.

"Why are you interested in our Master of Art program?"

I paused—trembling. Such a simple question caught me off guard. Had I really thought this through? The chapel advertisement alone didn't suffice. I wasn't passionate about art. This was already ending poorly, but I had to press on.

"Well, I'm interested in getting a master's degree and art is the closest thing to my studies."

The dean leaned in to me. "Oh, really? And what would that be?"

"Computer science."

He slumped back into his chair, clasping his hands. "That's not really . . . related to art."

I was losing the battle of wits. I had to think of a comeback. "I'm enrolled in the e-business minor. Half of it is art classes."

The dean returned a half smile. It was as if he could smell a phony a mile away. "And you think that qualifies you for the Master of Art program?"

I brainstormed—trying to keep confident. He was the dean of art. I knew nothing about the art programs at the college. I began pondering my e-business classes. "Well, I currently have an 'A' in Graphic Design."

"Good for you," he said. His stern stare remained. "Have you ever taken a drawing or painting class?"

I was failing this interview with my every word. Sure, I had a few basic drawing sessions in my school, but nothing formal. Besides kid art, my only painting experience was of a horse in a paint-by-numbers set when I was eight. Still, I had to think of something.

"Well, I took Conceptual Design last semester. That had some drawing and painting in it."

His piercing gaze continued to weigh me down. "I don't think you understand. We're talking about art at the *master's* level. This is an *intense* program that requires a lot of *serious* art skills."

I couldn't allow my ego to die that easily. "I *assure* you I can *do* this."

The man sighed, pondering for a moment. Reaching for his briefcase, he ruffled through some papers within. Pulling out a sheet, he began scratching at it with a shiny pen. Perhaps I'd finally earned his favor.

"You seem like you're confident enough, so I'll cut you a deal." He handed me the paper. It was a list of art classes with half of them circled. "If you take these classes and manage to get an 'A' in *all* of them, talk to me and I'll get you enrolled."

I was thrilled until I discovered the timeline—about two more years of coursework stood before me. I was already six years in as an undergraduate—more than ready to jump into a master's program. It was an offer I had to refuse.

I left the office dejected—my dreams of becoming a master artist crushed. With no other master's program in mind, I was out of luck. All that was left for me was a semester more of the e-business minor to sort things out.

Two days later, something unexpected happened that changed my life. During a morning chapel service, a professor of business announced a brand new master's program—business administration (MBA). It was to begin the following fall—the semester after my e-business minor would finish. Not only was this more intriguing to me than art, but I'd already completed more business classes than art classes.

In contrast to my appointment with the dean of art, my visit with the dean of business went swimmingly. All I lacked were four business classes—three of which fit into my final semester of e-business. The remaining one would be scheduled into my first semester in the graduate assistant contract. This time, I was actually going to become somebody!

CHAPTER 9

The Passerby

It was the fall of 2005 and I was halfway into finishing the MBA. Of course, the college had me working in the grounds department for my graduate assistant contract. Fortunately, for every semester, I had a steady 7:00 a.m.–11:00 a.m. Monday–Friday work schedule—much more organized and convenient than that of my classmates.

What had begun as my usual weeding and mowing responsibilities during undergraduate eventually morphed into a brand new unique responsibility. The first two hours of my day were replaced with trash duty around the borders of the campus. For the other two hours, I was put in charge of finding, distributing, and reporting miscellaneous garden maintenance tasks around campus. Little did my supervisor know that giving a computer science graduate access to a well-known piece of database office software would change the task reporting process for the better.

Within a week of managing the reporting of tasks at my office computer, I had secretly developed a task creation and reporting system. Once my supervisor caught a glance of what I had coded, he called the grounds manager and other supervisors over to see me demonstrate my application. They were impressed. After that, supervisors had me develop it into a full-fledged task creation and reporting system. They also had me create an employee problem reporting system and an equipment logging system to go along with it.

During my morning trash duty, I'd encounter interesting characters from right outside the campus borders. Some passersby would ask me what I was doing while others mocked me. Some, in a drunken stupor, would stagger up to me and claim that they'd seen me at the bar yesterday. Most of these individuals I'd only encounter once. However, one passerby had captured my curiosity by making a daily visit.

"Hello, sir." A polite middle-aged man would greet and salute me as he'd pass me by every morning, usually from the opposite side of the road.

"Hello, sir." I'd return his salute. As this positive daily encounter went on for a month, I gained an appreciation for it. It was the little things in life that could brighten up the day.

One evening, as I was exploring a dresser drawer in my room for its contents, a pile of gospel tracts jumped out. I think they may have waved to me.

"Give us out!" they seemed to be calling to me.

"Sure," I replied. "I know just the guy who might appreciate one of you." Why am I having a mental chat with a *pile of tracts*?

The next morning, I slipped a few of the tracts into my pocket before heading to my trash-picking crusade once again. Within the first hour, an old man began to approach from behind. Without thinking, I pulled out a tract and held it out to my side.

As he passed me from behind, he swiped the pamphlet from my hand and continued several paces. After glancing at it for a moment, he tucked it into his pocket and continued his trek.

"Score!" I said to my remaining buddies in my pocket. "We still need to be on the lookout for 'Hello, sir' out there." *Why was I talking to tracts again?*

It couldn't have been more than three minutes later when a familiar face appeared over the horizon. He was on the opposite side of the road, but he'd be crossing over to my path shortly. I had to remain busy without blowing this opportunity. The ground at my ten-foot radius must have been clean enough to eat off of when the passerby finally made it to me.

"Hello, *sir*," he greeted.

"Hello, sir." I saluted back, holding out my hand. "By the way, my name's John. What's yours?"

"Chris," he said, shaking my hand. He appeared startled, probably taken back by my sudden engagement after all this time.

"I've seen you walk past me every morning." I said.

"Yeah, I know," Chris laughed. "So, what are you doing here, anyways?"

"I work at the college as a graduate student. I clean the borders every morning."

"Oh, so *that's* what you're doing. I've always wondered why you're here every morning with that orange vest."

"Well, hey, Chris, I have something for you." Nervously digging in my pocket, I pulled out a tract and offered it. "Promise me you'll read it."

"I promise," he said, slipping it into his pocket. "Have a good day, sir."

"You, too."

The anxiety was over—mission complete. Would he actually read it? Would he actually believe the gospel? *Could this be my "divine appointment?"* I had to find out.

The following morning, I rushed to the same spot as before, giving it the cleaning of a lifetime. Like clockwork, Chris began to pass by.

"Hello, *sir*," he said.

"Good morning, Chris," I replied as he continued his trek. I wasn't going to let him get away that easily. "So, Chris, did you read that tract I gave you?"

Chris paused and thought a moment. "Uh . . . yeah."

"Did you ask Jesus to save you?"

"Uh . . . yeah."

"Then that means you're going to heaven, right?"

"Uh . . . yeah."

"Great!" I cheered.

"I appreciate it, man. Thanks a lot."

As he departed, I did all I could do not to burst into laughter. Had he read the tract and actually believed the gospel, he would've been eager to tell me about it, not trying to walk away. At least I tried.

The daily "Hello, *sir*" encounters with Chris continued for another week, but, after that, I never saw him again.

CHAPTER 10

The Curious Couple

I t had been a week since Chris had disappeared from the picture, but I continued to get my fill of daily passersby during my morning border cleanses. This particular day, at the same place where Chris used to cross, I looked back. A scraggly couple was approaching.

The man appeared to be in his late twenties with messy hair and facial stubble. The woman by his side could have been his mother. Both seemed overly dressed for the fall weather—thick, brown coats and beanie caps. Unlike the usual characters I'd encounter, they were different. I sensed warmth as they approached.

"Please, sir, could you spare a little change?" said the woman, placing her mitten-covered hands on my golf cart. "I'm really hungry and I just need a sandwich."

The man jolted a nervous glare at me—surprised by his companion's request. If this was an attempt to con me out of money, it was the most convincing acting I'd ever seen.

"What are you doing?" the man whispered to her. "Don't bother him." He pulled her hands off the cart. "Sorry about that," he said to me.

The two continued their walk; the man was still shocked by his companion. As I observed the duo, I grew more convinced that the act was genuine. Checking my wallet, I found no cash to spare. Consumed with guilt, I had to intervene.

"Wait!" I shouted.

The couple paused, then turned back to face me. They appeared more embarrassed than anything else.

"I just wanna let you know that I wish I could give you some cash, but I don't have any on me." I showed them the empty wallet. "All I have is cards. If you really need some cash, I could go back to the campus ATM for you."

The two smiled at each other then glanced warmly back—the woman returning an endearing, motherly smile.

"Aww, that's so sweet of you," she said, "but you don't have to do that."

"Yeah," the man added. "Don't worry about it. We don't want to trouble you."

Remembering my encounter with Chris, I figured it would be an opportunity to hand them a gospel tract. Alas, I didn't bring any! It looks like it was all me that moment. Perhaps a "divine appointment" was at hand.

"I do have a question for you," I said. "Do you know for sure if you're going to heaven?"

"Yes, sir," the man grinned.

I never expected a passerby to answer that with such confidence. I was intrigued. I had to prod further. "Oh, really? Could you tell me how to get to heaven?"

"You just gotta believe in Jesus!" the woman preached.

This was getting interesting. I had to know what this couple really believed. "Oh, really? Believe *what* about Jesus?"

"Believe that he died for your sins," the lady proudly proclaimed.

"Yes," I said. "It has nothing to do with your works. It's all about your faith in what Jesus did for you."

"Yeah, man," her companion added. "Too many people think they can earn their way to heaven. Even some people who call themselves Christians think that. They're wrong about that, man.

It has nothing to do with your works. It has everything to do with your faith in Jesus."

"Amen!" I cheered. "So, you're saved and going to heaven?"

"Yes, sir," he confidently affirmed.

We stood, smiling at each other for a moment.

"Well, hey, you have a great day," the man said. "I don't wanna interrupt your work. Thank you so much for talking to us."

I waved farewell to the couple. Mixed feelings about the encounter consumed me that day. It was the warmest encounter I'd ever had with any of the passersby, but I wished I had cash with me that moment. With a little sandwich money, I could have concocted a beautiful illustration of the love that Jesus had for them. Instead, I was nothing to them but words of encouragement.

CHAPTER 11

The Plan

G raduation was, once again, around the corner. In less than a month, I'd lose my job and my home. At this point, a piece of cardboard, "Will work for food" inscribed on it, was shaking over my head. Wait, *what*? My life had just come to *this*?

"This'll be John Mynyk under the bridge soon unless he agrees to sign a staff contract to work grounds."

OK, good. I wasn't the one holding the cardboard. It was the grounds manager. He was teasing me in my office.

"Have you gotten accepted into IT yet?" he prodded further.

"Not yet," I said.

He was playing games with me. About two weeks ago, I told him that I had filled out an application to work in the IT department. I just hadn't gotten a response yet.

"Well, we could always use you in grounds," he added. "We all have fun here on staff."

"I'm sure you do," I said.

But I hadn't spent eight years in college learning computer programming and business to end up pulling weeds for a living! Even if I were to do border cleaning and office application and database programming, that wasn't worthy of my education. All of that hard work in college wasn't about to fade into obscurity.

With no response yet to my request, I was in a panic. Eight years of college life was about to expire; convocation was rapidly approaching. I wasn't ready to move on without an IT contract. How tragic! It happens to the best of us.

With Daniel still working in the IT department, I wanted to join him and stay a little longer. However, I wanted to take advantage of the steady hours, low rent, and convenience of it being on the college campus. It was the perfect time to earn a doctoral degree.

The idea bonked me in the head during my first semester in the master's program. Both professors often discussed their doctoral dissertations. It's funny how such discussions, boring to my classmates, managed to excite me. I actually wanted to delve into a dissertation and write one myself; I wanted to be a part of that club.

My three goals were as follows:

1. Get a staff contract in the IT department.
2. Learn real-world coding skills on the job.
3. Earn a regionally accredited online doctoral degree.

It was all or nothing. If I didn't get the IT contract, I'd leave immediately. If I did get the contract but ended up coding mostly in an obsolete language, I'd leave once the contract ended in 2008. If I couldn't get accepted into a doctoral program, I'd also leave in 2008.

For the last month, I had religiously checked my campus mailbox daily for that IT contract. With about three weeks remaining until graduation, something floated down from heaven and landed in that little cubbyhole behind the combination lock. It was finally here! Dreams do come true!

Although my manager in grounds wasn't as thrilled about the news, my anxiety was over. I put in my best last three weeks of work in grounds and transitioned into IT.

CHAPTER 12

The Profession

It was Tuesday, June 6, 2006—the first day of my professional IT career and the infamous 06/06/06 date. Armed with new dress clothes and a Donald Trump Signature Collection tie I had purchased at a discount the previous weekend, I was ready to begin. Would anything evil happen on that unusual date on staff? I'd have to find out.

There I stood outside the manager's office—my heart racing. Within minutes, I'd discover my new job, boss, and coworkers for at least the next two years. It was all just a door knock away.

"Come on in," an inviting voice emanated from beyond.

Creaking the door open, I gazed upon a kind and gentle middle-aged man occupying the desk. He looked familiar. I'd seen him occasionally wandering around campus; he used to work as a networking technician years ago. Peering over his reading glasses, he smiled.

"Hi. I'm Mr. Tyler. What can I do for you?"

"Hi. My name's John Mynyk. This is my first day on staff as a programmer."

"Oh, yes, Mr. Mynyk," the man chuckled. He peered at a document. "We have you in . . . the Academy division. You're gonna be working for Jake. Do you have any questions for me before you begin?"

"Yes, I do. I wanna gain experience in modern and relevant technology. Is there a way to guarantee that?"

"Well, I can't guarantee you anything, but I think you'll be doing a lot of web and database programming. Does that interest you?"

"Sounds great!"

"As you might already know, we still use an old mainframe system, so you might also be working with that. Is that OK with you?"

"No problem," I assured him. "As long as I gain experience in modern web and database programming, that would be fine. Should I ever leave, I don't wanna have only experience with a mainframe that no one else uses."

"Perfectly understandable." The manager smiled. "Any more questions?"

"Nope. I'm ready to begin."

After meeting the IT staff, I found myself in my new desk, getting acquainted with my coworker; I was ready to begin . . . something.

"Hi, John. I'm Jake, your new boss." The man across from me shook my hand. "Welcome to the Academy division. Do you have any questions for me?"

"Sure. What would you like me to do?"

"Uh . . . let's see." He began searching his desk. A black binder more than half a foot thick plopped onto my desk. Jake slapped his hands on top of it, a grin plastered across his face. "You could start by reading the mainframe manual."

My heart skipped a beat. I had to read the entire manual? Was I going to become one of the mainframe-only developers? Is it too late to end my contract?

Assuring myself that the mainframe would be a side hustle, I snatched up the binder and began reading. It certainly wasn't the most exciting thing I'd ever read. Lunch could not come soon enough to jolt me out of my drowsiness.

After a hearty meal, I dove back into the black binder, unsure if I had remembered anything from it so far. Within an hour, I sensed a presence shadowing me from above. It was Jake, grinning down at me like he could taste my boredom.

"So, did you read through the whole manual yet?" he asked.

"Not yet. I think I got through about one-fifth of it."

"Well, you can put it away for now. I've got a project for you to work on."

It wasn't the mainframe's proprietary programming language. It was a website written in a modern programming language!

"So, what's the mainframe manual for?" I asked.

"It's for maintaining the old homeschooling sites. We do all our new stuff in the modern language."

"Cool. So, I take it the mainframe isn't all we do?"

"No," Jake chuckled.

It looks like the 06/06/06 date actually got off to a good start. I'd be learning in-demand programming skills. However, my final goal—enroll in a doctoral program—wasn't going to happen overnight.

That evening, I embarked on a university shopping spree online—applying for every regionally accredited online doctoral program I could find. About three days later, my campus mailbox was stuffed to the brim with university brochures. If my mailbox thought it had it bad, my cellphone was comparing notes—being assaulted daily by university recruiters.

Chapter 13

The Enrollment

As I had anticipated, getting enrolled in a regionally accredited online doctoral program wasn't going to be a cakewalk. Every day for the next two months, I received calls from academic recruiters offering doctoral programs in all kinds of studies such as business administration, education, and professional counseling. The one thing preventing enrollment was that my previous degrees didn't meet accreditation requirements at the time (PCC wouldn't become accredited until four years from now). Once that was uncovered, a recruiter would offer a bachelor's program instead.

Dejected, I visited the office of academic affairs one day during my lunch break. After relaying my situation to the man behind the desk, Mr. Greene, I asked him for advice.

"Take a look at these." He smiled, handing me brochures from three different universities.

These pamphlets had never touched my mailbox, but the schools' reputations and doctoral programs grabbed my attention. They offered a vast selection of doctoral programs.

"I like this one," I said, pointing to a brochure. "It offers business administration and it's 100 percent online."

"Are you absolutely sure you wanna enroll in that university?"

"Why?" I asked. "Is there something wrong with it?"

"Not at all," he said. "It's just that it might be the hardest of the three to get you into. If you really wanna get enrolled into that one, I'll do everything I can, but I can't guarantee anything. You'll probably have a better chance of getting into the other two."

"I could just reach out to all three and take the first one that accepts me."

"You could do that, but could I make a recommendation?"

"Sure."

He pointed to the one for University of Phoenix.

"University of Phoenix has an articulate agreement to accept our graduates," he said. "If you apply to this one, I can guarantee I'll get you enrolled. If a recruiter gives you any issues with the enrollment, just have 'em call me and I'll take care of it."

"Thank you, sir! I'll look into that."

That evening, I went onto the University of Phoenix enrollment website and filled out the application for doctor of business administration. Two days later, I received a call from a female recruiter. It was the first recruiter willing to walk me through the enrollment process. I was ecstatic!

Almost every day for the following month, I answered this lady's calls. I did everything she told me: write a letter of intent, obtain letters of recommendation from three professors, fax transcripts from my previous degrees, and fill out application forms. Everything seemed to be going smoothly.

"Congratulations! You've completed the entire enrollment process!" the voice cheered to me from over the phone one day in November. Her voice went silent for a moment. A sigh of disappointment followed. "There's just one problem keeping you from getting enrolled."

"What's that?" My heart skipped a beat.

"Your previous degrees don't meet our accreditation requirements."

We both went silent for half a minute. Not this again! Should I just give up?

"Is there anything you can do?" I begged. "I really wanna enroll in this doctoral program!"

"I know you do," she said. "Do you know if your college is planning to get accredited anytime soon?"

"Not that I know of."

"Then I don't know what else I can do for you," the lady sympathized. "That's a shame. We worked together on this whole process for so long only to have it end like this."

We both sighed together for a moment, unsure what to do to cheer each other up.

"*If a recruiter gives you any issues with the enrollment, just have 'em call me and I'll take care of it,*" Mr. Greene's voice echoed in my mind that moment. A glimmer of hope rushed through me.

"Would you like to talk to our *academic advisor*?" I said. "I remember him telling me that you actually accept graduates from our college."

"Oh, really?" The recruiter giggled. "That's interesting. Do you have his number?"

I swiped the little staff directory booklet off my desk and located Mr. Greene's number.

"OK," she said—her tone perked. "I hope this works, John, because this is our last attempt to get you enrolled. I'll call him and then I'll call you back within a few minutes with the conclusion."

May my work computer forgive me for the next few minutes; I couldn't utter another line of code. My hand gripped my cellphone—stunned—awaiting a life-changing vibration. Five minutes later, it buzzed.

"Hello?" I said.

"Congratulations, John!" the familiar voice cheered. "You're officially enrolled in the doctoral program! *Are you excited?*"

"Yes, I am! What happened in your call with Mr. Greene?"

The recruiter laughed. "It turns out your college *does* have an articulate agreement with us to accept their graduates. I guess you're all set. Congratulations once again!"

After ending the call, I dialed Mr. Greene's number to inquire.

"That was an easy call." He laughed. "I just told her that we have an articulate agreement with them. She then looked into that and found it to be true. I just love those kinds of calls."

The anxiety was over. I had two months left to relax before my life would be overtaken with schoolwork once again. Within that time, my new academic advisor called, offering me the chance to switch from the Doctor of Business Administration program to the Doctor of Management of Information Systems and Technology program. I thanked her for the offer and accepted; I didn't know that option was available. Could there have been more support for my life's goals than this?

CHAPTER 14

I'll Be Home Alone for Christmas

I n 1943, James Kimball Gannon wrote the famous Christmas song called "I'll Be Home for Christmas." Its perspective is from a soldier in World War II writing a letter to his family announcing his arrival home for Christmas, expecting to have the usual traditional celebrations. The ending sentence "I'll be home for Christmas, if only in my dreams" may convey the idea that the soldier either knows that he won't make it home or is not quite sure he will.

To a much lesser degree, I could relate during the years 2008 and 2009. During my entire three and a half years of doctoral classes, a one-week period surrounding Christmas was the only time I had off from both work and classes. Because I was behind on my doctoral dissertation, every bit of free time like that to work on it was precious. This was a time when everyone on campus would be gone to celebrate Christmas with their families. Sure, I was at home sweet home, if, by that, I mean dwelling alone in my PCC staff apartment dormitory room instead of visiting family.

It was a ghost town on the campus of PCC. There were no people, no cars, and no heat supplied to the dormitories. Fortunately, the college was courteous enough to supply electricity to the staff apartments just in case anyone remained. My fondest memories were those days I spent in silence, swaddled in my blankets, shivering, hearing only the tapping of my fingers on the keyboard.

Christmas day was my moment of peace and serenity; I took that day off from everything in its honor; it was my day to take an hour walk around campus, taking in the unique silence. All that remained were Christmas decorations—remnants of celebrations from weeks past. Not even the birds were there to sing Christmas carols. The silence was golden. If I didn't know any better, I'd say that a rapture occurred; I was left behind.

Did my two weeks of Christmas breaks writing my dissertation bear fruit? I wish I could say "Yes." After all, I did engage in extensive research. I did generate at least thirty pages. What went wrong? After my dissertation chair reviewed my work, I concluded it was useless—scrapping it and starting over.

My doctoral program was designed to take three and a half years to complete—assuming the dissertation could be worked in along with the classes. However, complications with my dissertation added two extra years to that. By the summer of 2009, Daniel had gotten married and moved to Colorado. With myriads more of software development jobs available in Colorado, my plan was to move there after I graduated. However, a "divine appointment" was brewing for me in Florida and I needed to stay for it. I just didn't know about it yet.

CHAPTER 15

The Bible Club

S omething was swimming around, searching for fresh blood. At least that's what I thought. Is that a fin in the water or are my eyes *deceiving* me? No! That's a fin! That's definitely a fin! It's coming closer! There's no way this boat will protect me from its powerful jaws!

Suddenly, the creature leapt out in front of me, opened its mouth wide and . . .

"Would you like to help me out in Bible Club this Saturday?"

Fortunately, it wasn't a shark. It was my friend Wayne, a fellow computer science graduate and IT worker. He was looking for fresh blood to help out in his ministry.

Wayne had inherited a children's ministry in 2001 called Bible Club, managing it ever since. Daniel and his girlfriend had faithfully helped him with the ministry during 2007 and 2008 before they moved to Colorado and got married in June of 2009. It was several months later. With two down, he was looking for replacements.

"Sure, I guess," I reluctantly agreed.

I was still involved in daily homework and weekend research papers; volunteer work hadn't even crossed my mind. I relayed to Wayne my concerns.

"I completely understand," he said. "If I ever ask you and you refuse, I won't be offended."

Bible Club took place in a local park Saturdays from 10:00 a.m. until 1:00 p.m. On the days I'd attend, I'd meet Wayne at his apartment at 9:00 a.m. to pack the needed supplies, ride in his car to pick up a few boys on the way to the park, and then help clean up the park grounds. I'd sweep the pavilion and pick up trash before the rest of the children arrived.

The regular schedule was as follows:

1. 10:00–10:59 a.m.—Free time for everyone to play sports, color in coloring books, play jump rope, or chat.

2. 11:00–11:59 a.m.—Regular Bible Club ministry activities.

3. 12:00–12:30 p.m.—Clean up time and more free time to play.

The hour of ministry time would be as follows in the park pavilion:

1. Congregational singing of a few Christian songs from printed visuals.

2. A memory verse erasing game; the children would repeat the memory verse from a whiteboard as Wayne would erase one word at a time until they could recite it together from memory.

3. An opening prayer.

4. A Bible lesson from a published children's Sunday school curriculum that included large, colorful, illustrative posters.

5. An attempt for children to recite the memory verse individually to earn a piece of candy.

6. Every first-time visiting or third-time regularly attending child would receive a toy from a wooden treasure chest.

At around 1:00 p.m., Wayne, other Bible Club staff, and I would clean, pack up our supplies, and walk some of the local children back to their houses. Once all of the local children returned home safely, I'd ride with Wayne in his car to return the few boys we picked up back to their homes, return to Wayne's apartment to unpack his Bible Club supplies, and then I'd return to my apartment.

For the first year at Bible Club, I attended only once a month due to my homework demands. Upon completing my last class sometime in April or May of 2010, I began attending Bible Club every Saturday as I worked on my dissertation.

CHAPTER 16

Moving Off Campus

" *C lick!*"—the last class assignment ever just got sent onto the information superhighway to be graded. The tyranny of daily schoolwork and monthly tuition was finally over—only the dissertation remained. At that point, I desired to live in a quieter apartment while I worked on my dissertation—one not owned by and located on PCC's campus.

PCC's campus had been my home since I was eighteen years old. It was now around the end of March of 2010—I'd turn thirty in less than two months. With tuition payments off the table, I could now afford an extra $200 or $300 per month to reside off campus. I could avoid the noises of people in the dorm halls as well as the random fire drills.

At the time, the college had an unwritten policy where unmarried men working for the college were to live on campus, but I'd heard of exceptions. Unaware of how to get an exception granted, I crafted a letter for the employment office one night, explaining my desire to move. I dropped it off at the office the following morning.

About a week later, as I was performing my daily campus mailbox inspection ritual, another piece of paper seemed to have floated down from heaven—my request had been granted. It set a scheduled date of exit from the dormitory toward the end of

May—about a week after my thirtieth birthday. With a reasonable scope of time to search for a new home, I began giving my computer and cellphone a run for their money to find a new place to rest my head.

One evening, while on a call with a college graduate and friend from out of state, I got the scoop on an exceptional apartment complex three miles from the campus. Finding the leasing office staff delightful and the rent reasonable, I established my new residence where I could finish my dissertation with fewer distractions.

CHAPTER 17

A Dissertation Proposed

L adies and gentlemen, welcome to the winter academic fight of 2010! From the red corner, weighing in at ninety pages of research, proposed data collection, and proposed data analysis, please welcome John Mynyk's dissertation proposal! And, from the blue corner, weighing in at about six weeks of dissertation-proposal-crushing review, please welcome Academic Review Board (ARB)! Fellows, I want a good clean match! Ready? Fight!

Proposal jumps into the ring swinging. It swings a grammar jab and a mechanics uppercut. Miss! Oooo! ARB delivers a denying blow to the chin! Proposal is down for the count!

One week! Two weeks! Three weeks! Four weeks! Five weeks! Six weeks! Ladies and gentlemen, Proposal is back up on its feet ready for another round! Patching up its grammar and mechanics injuries, it's ready, once again, to go in swinging! There's the bell for round two! Fight!

Proposal shows new vigor, swinging like a wild man! Oooo! ARB clocks him with a right denial hook to the face! Once again, Proposal is down for the count!

One week! Two weeks! Three weeks! Four weeks! Five weeks! Six weeks! This is remarkable, folks! Proposal is back on its feet— dazed! The fighters are now rested. Proposal has bandaged up its mechanical wounds it thought it had defended! There's the bell for round three! Fight!

Proposal is charging in like an eagle, going for its prey! Oooo! It locks three jabs and an uppercut! ARB is stumbling back! It hits the ropes! Oh! Proposal just took ARB down with a nasty right hook of grammar sufficiency! Ladies and gentlemen, ARB is out! It's completely out!

After eighteen weeks, Proposal has finally won! But that's not all, folks! A new challenger has just jumped into the ring! Is this even legal? Actually, it is! The new opponent is the Information Review Board (IRB), ready to challenge Proposal's legal standing in data collection! I guess Proposal has no choice but to accept. There's the bell for round one! Fight!

Proposal marches toward its smaller opponent with confidence. Armed with a fool-proof legal data collection method, it can't lose! IRB comes in swinging like a child trying to get a Popsicle from his bullying big brother. Proposal places its hand down on IRB's forehead, holding him back as he continues swinging. Sorry, IRB, but Proposal is geared for a flawless victory. . . . Oooo! *What just happened?* IRB just connected with a leaping hook! Proposal is on its back! I guess its data collection legality wasn't as clear as it thought! It's down for the count!

One week! Two weeks! Three weeks! Proposal is up with a clearer clarity on its data collection legality! It marches toward IRB with renewed vigor! IRB attempts a second leaping hook! Proposal ducks! Oooo! Proposal just connected with a right cross! *Is that it?* IRB is out! All hail the new champion, Proposal! It was a grueling twenty-four weeks, but Proposal finally fought its way to victory!

CHAPTER 18

A Dissertation Completed

"Any intelligent fool can make things bigger, more complex, and more violent. It takes a touch of genius—and a lot of courage— to move in the opposite direction."

—ALBERT EINSTEIN

Unfortunately, I wasn't familiar with this wisdom from Albert Einstein when I had gotten my dissertation prospectus approved in 2007. Having a study with a simpler data collection method would have saved me time and money on this stage of the dissertation. However, if I did, the outcome of this story could have been different, rendering this book nonexistent.

"Your goal is not to save the world," a professor said to us in our 2009 residency. "Your goal is to finish your dissertation so that you can graduate as soon as possible."

In the 2009 residency, I had asked fellow students what their data collection method would be like. They all seemed to understand the KISS principle—keep it simple, stupid. Most of their data collection processes could happen in one hour, in one classroom, in one survey, or from one website.

Was my data collection process even near as simple as that of my peers? Not a chance! For my study, each person filling out my survey had to represent the IT department of a different company—a Fortune 500 company to be precise. Could all of *that* kind of data be collected in one *hour*? Once again, not a chance!

My first instinct was to get my hands on mailing addresses to the CEOs of Fortune 500 companies. At the time, the only way I could obtain such a list was to purchase one from some questionable-looking website for about one hundred dollars. Upon obtaining the list, I spent several hundred dollars on stamps from PCC's bookstore, printed 360 surveys, made out envelops to 360 different CEOs, and then dropped them into the college mail slot. I'd bet the postman got a surprise if he noticed 360 letters with the same return address.

Three months later, I had received five filled-out surveys by mail and three by email. About a hundred envelops came back with "return to sender—invalid address" written on them. Perhaps most of the Fortune 500 CEOs turned over since I bought the addresses. Perhaps the list of addresses hadn't been updated in a long time. Whatever the reason, I was not going to get 222 more filled-in surveys anytime soon unless I had changed my technique. My academic advisor was growing impatient.

My next approach was to try sending the surveys via LinkedIn InMails. I had to upgrade to LinkedIn Premium to get access to twenty-five InMails per month. The night I upgraded, I sent all twenty-five InMails to different CEOs. About two weeks later, I only received two filled-out surveys by InMail. That was ten down, only 220 more complete surveys to go to make my analysis statistically significant. There had to be a faster way to get results!

I found a popular surveying tool that claimed it would guarantee results . . . for a price. After a week of phone calls to the surveying company and taking a dent out of my wallet, 220 completed surveys happened. The tyranny of data collection was finally over.

I just needed professional software to do some statistical analysis on my data.

Having used a piece of software called Statistical Package for the Social Sciences (SPSS) a couple of times in my MBA classes, I figured I could rent the software just long enough to run the statistics. One evening, I searched online for SPSS student licenses. The pricing was beyond my pay grade, especially if I only needed it for about an hour. It soon dawned on me that I may be able to borrow access to it at PCC in a laboratory.

The next evening, I found a fellow professor of computer science in his office. Upon explaining my situation, he walked me into a computer lab and logged me into his SPSS account. That was extremely nice of him!

After an hour, I had successfully entered my data into SPSS, ran a backward stepwise regression analysis, then downloaded and printed the results. With the burden of data collection and analysis done that day, I got the best night's sleep I had in years. All the difficult parts of the dissertation were completed. I just had to write the data analysis chapter and the conclusion and recommendations chapter. There was nothing now holding me back except my own laziness.

Every evening for the next month, my computer keyboard got the workout of its life, keeping up with my drive to finish the draft. It was the beginning of the summer of 2012 when I had finally clicked that submit button on the university's website to send my completed draft over for review. All I could do now was wait for a response; I had no idea how long that would take.

Two weeks later, the results came back. It was not approved! Don't worry. It was rejected only for a few minor errors. I didn't have to strap on the gloves and duke it out like "Proposal" did when it fought ARB and IRB. The interesting thing was that I had a two-week summer vacation coming up to visit Daniel and his family in Colorado within about two days. I quickly made the corrections and resubmitted the draft.

With about two days remaining of my vacation, once again, something seemed to float down from heaven, but, this time, land in my email inbox.

"Congratulations! Your dissertation draft is approved. Just fix a few minor changes for publication and schedule a time with your dissertation chair and committee members for your oral defense."

Hyped with the news, I sent emails to my dissertation chair and committee to schedule the oral defense; we agreed to the conference call on Saturday morning, July 14 at 10:00 a.m.—several weeks later.

CHAPTER 19

An Oral Defense

It was a gray and drizzly Saturday morning. On July 14 of 2012, I leapt out of bed at 6:00 a.m. ready to do the oral defense of my dissertation and finish my doctorate once and for all. Try as they may, the gray clouds couldn't bring me down. In fact, they were welcome to listen in on my conference call if they wanted. Perhaps they could learn something.

After three more rehearsals of my script, I set up my video camera toward my computer screen and initiated my conference call. My dissertation chair joined and chatted about the weather. Fifteen minutes later, one of the two committee members joined in on the fun. After the other committee member joined five minutes later, the fear of potential rescheduling was over. I pushed the record button and began to speak.

After thirty minutes of speaking and twenty minutes of playing a game of "twenty questions," the conference call for me was over. Passing control to the dissertation chair, I left the call. I was stiffer than a statue—staring at my cellphone in anticipation. My heart couldn't stop racing.

Twenty minutes later, my cellphone finally rang.

"Congratulations, Dr. Mynyk!" the chairman cheered. "You passed your defense!"

It was what dreams were made of! Unfortunately, the nightmare wasn't quite over. One of the committee members refused to sign off on my dissertation. I needed at least four more citations from sources less than four years old.

My heart sank from mixed feelings. I had earned my title but not my freedom. There had to be a way to finish this final task quickly.

After browsing through my dissertation for a minute, I discovered a solution. There in the abstract and opening was a prominent statistic that had already been linked to multiple sources both recent and old. Within an hour, I did a quick literature review on the statistic and sources, adding four more to the citation.

About fifteen minutes later, my committee member emailed me a statement praising me for fulfilling his request quickly and signed off for approval. I was finally done! It was time to celebrate like how any good person would who has just completed a doctorate—go grocery shopping at Walmart, of course!

CHAPTER 20

A Failed Bible Lesson

I was finally done with my goals in Florida—gain valuable IT work experience and earn a regionally accredited doctorate. I was ready to move to Colorado. Unfortunately, I was bound by a work contract. I couldn't just get up and go.

The contract had to be renewed every year during January. Every renewal had to last at least a year but always ended on August 1. Although I had finished my doctorate in July, I had already renewed my contract. Back in January, I had no idea that I would finish in July. Had I known that, I would not have renewed.

No big deal. I'd get to enjoy a little more than a year of work at the IT department without being enslaved to the tyranny of school. Wayne could use more help at Bible Club.

For the remainder of my contract, Bible Club was my ritual every Saturday morning. Of course, being the introvert that I was, all I did was play games with the children and clean up the park. I thought I could slip by without ever leading a song or teaching a Bible lesson. However, life never lets one coast by in a rut.

"John, I know you've never taught any of the lessons at Bible Club before," Wayne said to me at work one afternoon, "but I'm going on vacation next week and I know you're planning to be here. Could you teach the lesson next week on the nativity?"

This happened in the middle of December of 2012. My doctorate was already finished. Looks like I had no excuses for getting out of this one.

"Sure," I reluctantly agreed.

"I know teaching isn't your thing, but I'm sure you can handle it."

I pondered the lesson that evening in my apartment. If I was going to teach my first lesson, it couldn't be some boring portrayal of the nativity story. It had to be worthy of the name John Mynyk!

I did some research and watched some unusual and controversial videos on the nativity, conjuring up as much fascinating data as I could in my notes.

That Saturday, I came in confident, ready to blow everyone away with my "edutainment" lesson on what "really happened" at the nativity.

Was it the best Bible lesson the children had ever heard at Bible Club? Not by a long shot! It was the most embarrassing speech I'd ever done in my life. My confidence was down. My cadence was all over the place. Children were making faces at me and I wasn't even offended. I could feel their pain. If this was the best Bible lesson I could do, I'd hate to see my worst.

After Wayne returned to work two weeks later, I conveyed to him the failure of my Bible lesson. Assuming I was just being too hard on myself, he politely accepted my concerns and refrained from asking me to teach again. Perhaps a failed Bible lesson was the proof I needed to return to my usual minimal roles. However, a plot had hatched in my mind to redeem myself someday with a better Bible lesson delivery.

CHAPTER 21

A Conflict of Contracts

My work contract was finally nearing an end. It was June of 2013. My contract was ending on August 1. In my mind, I'd be on the road then and arrive at Daniel's house in Colorado by August 5. I decided to head over to my apartment leasing office to tell them that I'd be leaving soon.

"It really makes us sad to see our occupants leave us," the girl at the desk said with a sigh. She had gotten to know me over the last three years and developed a small crush.

"I know. I really enjoyed my stay here," I said. "These are wonderful apartments."

"I'm glad you like them. So, your contract ends November 15."

My heart skipped a beat. I couldn't afford to take a three-month vacation without a job.

"*November 15?* My work contract ends August 1!" I said. "Is there any way you can let me off earlier?"

"Sorry, but if you leave earlier, we're gonna have to charge you rent for the time you missed plus a lease-breaking fee."

She added up all the fees. Of course, it was more than I had saved up at the time.

"I'll see if I can request a three-month extension to my work contract," I said.

"I hope you can get that straightened out."

Upon returning to my apartment, I cursed the day I wrote that letter to ask for permission to move off campus. Had I remained on campus, I wouldn't have to worry about extending my contract or getting a temporary job for three months. Perhaps God was chastising me for moving off campus for selfish reasons. I didn't even think about how my work contract's end date wouldn't synchronize with my apartment lease end date.

I prayed, apologizing for my selfishness. I prayed for a three-month extension to my contract to be granted, but had my doubts. I had never, at this point, heard of any stories of employees at PCC asking for a small contract extension to know if it was plausible. The last thing I wanted was to get a minimum-wage job serving fast food and still not quite earn enough to pay the rent. I feared that God could even have a sense of humor and want to "teach me a lesson" for moving off campus by giving me a night shift to top it off. All I could do that night was to keep apologizing for my selfishness and plead for a contract extension.

The following morning, I marched over to the campus information desk to pour out my plea for mercy.

"Hello. How may I help you?" asked the young lady standing behind the desk.

I unloaded to her my apartment leasing situation and my dire need for an extra three months added to my work contract.

"Hmmm . . ." the young lady said, pondering her response. "We don't really . . . do that . . . here . . . so . . . we have no forms like that for you to fill out. . . . I'm . . . not sure how to . . . help you . . . with that."

I sighed in disgust, glaring helplessly into her eyes.

"I tell you what," she said with a grin. "Why don't you write a letter to the employment office explaining your situation? I'm not sure if they'll grant your request, but it's worth a try."

"Thanks. I'll try that."

That evening, my computer's keyboard got a workout once again. I crafted the most humble and urgent letter I could to convey my request for a contract extension. After dropping off the letter to the employment office the next morning, I let Mr. Tyler know of my concerns.

"Well, John," he said, "it'd be great if we could have you for three more months, but I'm not sure if they'll grant your contract extension. They just don't do that kind of thing around here."

I'd never felt such helplessness and anxiety. More than ever, I needed another memo to float down from heaven into my mailbox. Each day, Mr. Tyler would ask me if the extension was granted. Each day, I'd tell him no. Each day, he'd remind me that it's most likely not going to be granted. Each day, a minimum-wage night shift somewhere haunted my mind. Needless to say, concentration on my coding at work was increasingly becoming a chore.

The longer I waited for a memo to arrive, the less time I had to seek another job. However, if I sought another job too soon, I could end up getting hired somewhere else only to find out that my contract extension would get granted afterward. With two and a half weeks of my contract remaining, things were looking dire.

"This is for you, John." The IT secretary was doing her rounds delivering mail directly to employees' desks. I never figured out why some of the campus mail came to work instead of the mailbox. Apparently, I was a recipient to a memo. Could this be what I thought it could be?

"Haaaaallelujah!"

This memo floated down from heaven (or at least from the IT secretary) right onto my desk at work.

"Congratulations. Your request for an extension to your work contract has been granted. Your new contract end date is October 31."

The anxiety was gone! I ran into Mr. Tyler's office to proclaim the good news.

"That's great, John!" he cheered. "I'm really surprised they actually granted your request!"

What adventures would be in store for me during this three-month contract extension? Perhaps a "divine appointment?"

CHAPTER 22

Ministering on Borrowed Time

I t was August 3 of 2013—the first Saturday after the beginning of my work contract extension.

"Notice how we're past August 1 and I didn't resign my work contract in January, yet I'm still here." I relayed my story to Rachel—a regular helper and teacher at Bible Club.

"That's cool," said Rachel. "Well, we're glad to have you. Maybe God has a reason for you to remain here these three extra months."

It couldn't have been more than ten minutes later when a car arrived unexpectedly near the park entrance. Out popped two adorable young girls dressed as if coming from a 1950s sock hop; they both were wearing long, frilly, old-fashioned dresses and stilettos. The driver waved to them and took off. Without hesitation, the darling duo marched up to the pavilion, grabbed a Frisbee, and approached.

"Would you like to play catch with us?" the older one said.

"Sure," I said with a grin.

The two new visitors, Rachel, and I tossed the disk around for a minute without saying a word. I had to break the ice. "I'm John, by the way. What are your names?"

"I'm Amy," the older one said, "and this is my sister Holly."

"Nice to meet you, Amy and Holly," Rachel politely greeted. "How old are you?"

"I'm eight," Amy said, "and Holly's seven."

"Wow," Rachel added. "Well, we're glad to have you. So, how did you hear about this place?"

"Well, we didn't actually *hear* about this place," Amy said. "Our mom wanted to run an errand. On her way, she saw this park full of kids and figured she could drop us off."

"Oh, wow," said Rachel. "Well, we're glad to have you with us. What we do here is called 'Bible Club.' You missed it today, but we come here every Saturday morning at ten. We play games, we memorize Bible verses, we sing songs, and we teach Bible stories. Would you like that?"

"Yeah," said Amy. "That sounds fun."

Within the next hour, the children finished their playtime and headed home. Rachel and I continued our game of catch with the two new guests until their ride arrived.

"Well, that was fun," I said to Rachel. "I hope they actually come back."

"Yeah," she said. "I sure hope nobody tries to pick them up and take them away, because they are just too precious."

What an interesting first Bible Club of my work contract extension. It allowed me to meet two friendly new girls at Bible Club. Could this three-month period of "borrowed time" be a so-called "divine appointment?" Stay tuned!

CHAPTER 23

Return of the Guests

"Amy and Holly, you decided to come back!" I shouted to our beloved new guests as they ran up to greet me again.

It was the following Saturday morning—August 10. By their attire, it wasn't a sock hop they were coming from, but rather Woodstock—tattered jeans, tie-dye shirts, and a necklace with a peace-sign pendant.

"Yes, we're back!" Amy said with a laugh. Reaching in the supplies bag, she retrieved a plastic orange ball and toy road cones. "Would you like to play catch with me . . . with *this*?"

"Sure."

"Let's see if we can catch the ball in these cones," she said.

"And also throw it from the cones?" I asked.

"Sure, sounds like fun."

As Holly joined Rachel and other girls to do some coloring, Amy and I began playing our odd game of catch.

"So, Amy, I guess you're gonna be attending Bible Club regularly?" I asked.

"Yeah," she said. "We told our mom that we liked it here and wanted to come back. She doesn't seem to mind. I think it gives her some time to herself."

"I guess it's a win-win situation for everyone." I smiled.

"Yeah." Amy's smiled matched mine.

Attempting to catch Amy's ball in my cone, it bounced off, rolling on the grass.

"Oops," I joked, pretending to stumble around while fumbling with the ball.

"You know, Mr. John," Amy said, "you're a very funny man."

"Thanks. I'll take that as a compliment."

As we played catch for a minute, I couldn't help staring at Amy's colorful shirt. "Nice tie-dye and peace sign. It's quite cheery." I held up two fingers. "Peace."

"Peace," she said, smiling and matching my gesture.

A middle-aged man who joined us for lunch sometime the prior week volunteered to take the reins of today's Bible lesson. Being that he had never attended Bible Club, he was braver than I certainly was at volunteering for teaching Bible lessons.

Bible lessons at Bible Club were usually taught in a soft, exciting storytelling voice. Instead, this stranger preached as if he were Billy Sunday. The lesson escapes my memory, but, like a typical evangelist, he ended with an invitation to the gospel. To my delight, a little boy, Junior, between ages six to eight, raised his hand, indicating that he was unsure of his own salvation.

After the lesson, the children began their usual ritual of reciting the memory verse to earn a piece of candy. While assisting with the verse recitations, I heard the teacher lead the boy through a "sinner's prayer." Though I couldn't hear their words through the commotion, I saw the man rejoice that the boy had just received salvation. I was thrilled. I rarely saw such happen before my eyes.

Amy and I raced to the plastic ball and cones, continuing our catching game that was becoming oddly addictive. However, my eyes curiously leapt to observe our new convert; I wanted to see him rejoice in the Lord.

"Ouch! He hit me!"

Two boys were wrestling on the ground for a football.

"All right boys! Break it up!" the preacher rebuked, pulling the two apart. "Junior! Why'd you hit him? You know you're not supposed to punch people!"

"Because he took my ball and I wanted it back!" The boy pouted as he sat in the pavilion, folding his arms.

"Now, Junior," the preacher said, "hitting people is not nice. You shouldn't do that, especially since you just got saved. That's not how a Christian young man should be acting."

Junior glared at the ground, retaining his tempered countenance.

"Now, go apologize," said the preacher.

Reluctantly, the boy left his seat and made amends. At this moment, my mind entered a philosophy debate. If a boy had just discovered the "secrets of the universe" and the love of Jesus, why'd he be more focused on a football minutes later? Does this mean he didn't really believe the gospel, or was this still expected behavior for a young boy? It was one of life's mysteries.

CHAPTER 24

A Storm Now and Then

My one and only Bible lesson I had taught at Bible Club was a flop. Could I really leave for Colorado on that legacy? Each Saturday at Bible Club, I'd ponder another crack at teaching a lesson. Would a second lesson be better or worse than the first?

I had a good and relaxing routine at the park. Amy continued to play games of catch with me faithfully as well. I was too shy to glance at the lesson sign-up sheet. Any schedule gaps would present to me needless conviction. Perhaps cleaning the park and playing catch with Amy was good enough for me. If no one asked me to teach, I just figured there was no need.

Since Amy and Holly joined Bible Club, they had projected a peculiar fashion trend. They both wore similar outfits together, but they were dramatically different each week. They were obviously following a pattern. I didn't crack the code until about two years later. See if you notice it sooner:

- Week one—Fancy dresses with big collars and stilettos.
- Week two—Tattered jeans, tie-dye shirts, and peace signs.
- Week three—Simple t-shirts with hip-hugger bell-bottom jeans.

- Week four—Oversized neckhole colorful t-shirts.
- Week five—Colorful shirt and more loose-fitting jeans.

Notice the pattern? Does it not seem like a sequential progression through twentieth-century decades of clothing styles? Regardless of attire, they always acted the same—the sweetest, kindest, most respectful, and most mature children at Bible Club in my opinion.

"Peeeee-*yoo!*" a guest speaker proclaimed, teaching a Bible lesson on August 17 of 2013. It was a delightful man I had met a couple of times. He worked some staff position at PCC.

The lesson he taught that morning was from 2 Kgs 5. In it was the story of how Naaman, a mighty man of valor, received healing from his leprosy after obeying Elisha's command to dip himself seven times in the Jordan River.

With an energetic, childlike demeanor, the man brought smiles and laughter teaching this tale. As he'd mention Naaman's leprosy, he'd pinch his nose and playfully shout "Peeeee-*yoo!*" Understanding the difficulty of talking about leprosy to a bunch of children, I had to give this man credit. His antics and teaching style were hilarious and spot-on.

Contrasted to that cheerful, sunny day, the following Saturday saw the cries of thunder and gray skies. Despite the warnings, Wayne kept Bible Club on the schedule. After bringing the same two boys on our way to the park, Wayne and I soon found ourselves sheltered by the pavilion as we watched the clouds grow darker. The lady workers arrived just in time to join us before the downpour.

With seven adults and only three boys, Bible Club was looking uneventful. To increase the entertainment value, the boys did what boys do best—get filthy. For the next fifteen minutes, they rolled, flopped, and crawled around in the accumulating water puddles. Needless to say, they returned to the pavilion soaked and shivering. After drying them off with a towel, Wayne announced the end of Bible Club that day and began packing his belongings.

CHAPTER 25

A Second Chance

I t was Saturday, August 31, and the storm clouds were over once again. Amy and I continued our ritualistic game of ball-and-toy-road-cones catch. Amy, wearing her 1990s attire, decided to reflect to me a blast from the past. It dawned on me later that the song she kept singing to me during our game was from some early 1990s pop culture. I didn't pick up on her cues until reflecting on it while writing this book.

As I began helping pack up the supplies after Bible Club, Wayne approached me with that familiar face and tone he had from last December in the office. I knew what was coming next.

"Uh, John," he said, holding up the lesson sign-up sheet, "I hate to ask you this because I know you don't usually volunteer to teach the lessons."

Pointing toward a gap of empty slots on the schedule, he continued. "There's four weeks in a row here where no one has signed up. Normally, I do the lessons on the days no one volunteers, but four weeks in a row is just too much for me."

Wayne's face seemed to express immediate regret of his own ask. He was under too much pressure to teach the lessons. I couldn't put him through that.

I browsed through the gaps for something interesting. "Noah's Ark" on September 21 glared back. I wrote my name into the slot. Before I could put down the paper, Wayne offered me one last chance to retract my decision. I assured him that a chance to teach again was on my mind; I just needed the nudge.

Noah's ark would serve as my "swan song" for Bible Club and my remaining time in Florida. From that moment on, my mind was consumed with it. After returning from Bible Club, I retrieved the lesson's visuals from the campus library, returned to my apartment, and began typing an outline for the lesson.

After an hour, I was ready for a practice round. I snipped paragraphs out of my print, taped them to the back of the posters, and began teaching to an imaginary audience. Unfortunately, I sounded like a boring, stammering mumbler—my previous failure was rearing its ugly head.

After four more practice runs, I put the posters down, dejected. All I could see at that point were the mocking faces of the young audience returning. I was not going to leave for Colorado on that note. There had to be a way to save this lesson.

CHAPTER 26

Search the Scriptures

It was Saturday, September 7, and Bible Club was beginning a kickball fad. Instead of the usual gravitation of small groups of children to a variety of games or activities, all of the children wanted to play a game of kickball. It began before the main Bible Club events and continued afterward. Unfortunately for Amy and Holly, they had just recycled their attire back to the 1950s—long gowns and stilettos.

"It's hard to run in high heels," Amy huffed at me while hobbling along to third base.

"I can only imagine," I said, standing as an outfielder.

After Rachel taught a Bible lesson about Adam and Eve, most of the children and adults returned to finish the kickball game. However, Rachel, Amy, and two of the boys decided to do something else. Under the pavilion, Rachel and Amy took a seat at the table to chat. There was a lone book in the middle of the table that caught Amy's attention.

"Is that *your* Bible?" she asked.

"Yes, it is, Amy," said Rachel.

"May I look at it?"

"Sure."

I was captivated. I was never aware that the child had any interest in reading a Bible. I wanted to join them and start a conversation.

"Mr. John!" It was one of the boys to the left at the swing set. Two boys were glancing at me from the swings. One of them was holding a tennis ball.

"While we're swinging," one of them said, "you throw this ball at us. Try to get it as close to us as you can without it hitting us."

It seemed like a simple activity of amusement, but my attention was on Rachel, Amy, and the Bible. Amy's face was buried into the pages.

Like Paul in Phil 1:23–24, I was "in a straight betwixt two, having a desire to depart, and to be with Amy; which is far better: Nevertheless to abide in the tennis ball swing set game is more needful for the two boys." I wished I could be like Philip to the Ethiopian eunuch in Acts 8:30. I wanted to appear in front of Amy and ask, "Understandest thou what thou readest?" and see what would happen from there.

CHAPTER 27

A Friend's Approval

It was Saturday, September 14, the week after Amy and Holly wore their gowns. They were now due to return in their tie-dye shirts and peace-sign necklaces. Strangely enough, Amy decided to pick up the toy road cones and orange ball and ask me to play catch with her once again. *Was I experiencing déjà vu?*

"Hey, I remember that shirt," I said.

"This is my favorite outfit," Amy said, pointing at her shirt.

After a lady taught the lesson about Cain and Abel, I headed back near the pavilion to continue to play catch with Amy again like the last time she was dressed for Woodstock. To my surprise, she decided to join Rachel at the table and continue reading from her Bible. Like clockwork, the same two boys as last time pulled me away to play the tennis ball swing set game again until Wayne announced pack-up time.

As I was about to bag the lesson sign-up sheet, two little hands latched onto it. It was Amy; she began poring over it.

"So, who's doing the lesson next week?" she asked.

"Actually . . . *I* am," I said. I had never seen her look at the teaching schedule before or ask about the lessons.

"Oh, so *you're* doing the lesson?" Amy's grin grew.

"Yes, I am." I grinned back. "Wish me luck, because this isn't something I normally do."

"Cool, Mr. John! I'm looking forward to it!"

The pressure was on! My newfound friend and fan Amy was rooting for me. I couldn't let her down. Failure was no longer an option. My lesson had to be perfect . . . somehow.

CHAPTER 28

Saved by the Rain

B eep, beep, beep
I sighed in disgust, slapping the switch to turn off my alarm clock. Rarely did the thing ever wake me up. Most days I would awaken within five minutes prior to shut it off before it would alert me with its nagging beep. I must have been exhausted—perhaps from practicing my Bible lesson too much.

It was Saturday, September 21, 2013 at 7:00 a.m.—my chance to shine with a better delivery of a Bible lesson. I was groggy and unprepared. Still, I had one last chance to prove that I could pull it off. I picked up the posters and began my final practice run. I sounded like a tranquilized Herman Munster. It was worse than ever.

I began another practice round, pacing around the room and swinging my arms frantically. Perhaps I just needed more energy to break up the boredom. Alas, it also went down in flames. Two more quick rehearsals only proved one thing: my delivery grew worse every time.

It was time to accept my fate as a Bible teacher. If anything, I could prove to my friends and the children that John Mynyk should be seen and not heard. I gathered my lesson posters and slumped toward the door.

Just as my hand grasped the knob, my cellphone buzzed in my pocket.

"Hello?" I answered.

"Hi, John. This is Wayne. I'm just letting you know that I'm canceling Bible Club today because of the rain."

"The rain?" I cracked the door open and peeked out. The sun, a cloudless blue sky, and the chirping of birds greeted me back. "Are you sure it's gonna rain?"

"I think so," said Wayne. "I checked the weather and I think it's gonna rain. It probably won't, but I've already let everyone know that Bible Club is cancelled today."

The moment I ended the call, I could hear the hallelujah chorus echoing down on me from that blue sky outside. With a whole extra week to prepare my lesson, I was now free to do whatever I pleased at that moment. I could dive back into bed, which was my biggest temptation. I could go grocery shopping at Walmart. I could play a video game. I could watch a relaxing flick. The sky was the limit for an entire Saturday of freedom.

I walked toward my computer desk to plop the posters down for a break. I was failing my lesson because I was trying too hard anyways. Putting them down to enjoy the day off was necessary for improving the lesson later after a recharge.

As I reached down to drop the posters, I began to feel sorry for them. It was as if they were staring at me with exaggerated teary puppy dog eyes. I couldn't let them go without one more practice round.

With a clear mind free of the pressure of performing that day, something different happened. For the first time ever, I was actually satisfied with my performance. It was a miracle! The rain that never happened had just saved my lesson!

CHAPTER 29

Ishbibenob Slays the Crowd

C hatter was all over the place as the auditorium filled up for another church service. I sat in a chair on the far-left section—affectionately referred to as "the shelf." I had never sat in this section. From this ninety-degree angle, I'd be looking directly at the preacher's right profile. Most of the choir wouldn't be visible, nor would the gargantuan screen behind them displaying the service from the view of the broadcasting cameras.

It was Wednesday evening, September 25, 2013. In three days, I'd be unleashing Enoch and Noah on the unsuspecting children at Bible Club. I sat in the church chair, anticipating Saturday morning's outcome. Having practiced every night, I noticed a decline in my performance since last Saturday when the rain that never was rescued me from failure.

I contemplated leaving—heading back to my apartment for another practice round. Perhaps God would understand if I skip this church service. After all, I had a more pressing matter to attend to in his honor—improving my lesson and assuring Amy's satisfaction. A single Wednesday evening service couldn't be more important.

To my surprise, my favorite guest speaker marched up to the pulpit. I hadn't seen him in at least two years. One thing I did remember from his last appearance was a sermon that had the audience roaring with laughter. There was no chance he'd resurrect such a sermon today, would he?

"Our text is from 2 Sam 21:15–22," the guest preacher said. "'Moreover the Philistines had yet war again with Israel; and David went down, and his servants with him, and fought against the Philistines: and David waxed faint. . . . And . . . Ishbibenob . . .'"

There it was. As soon as he said "Ishbibenob," I knew he was resurrecting his classic sermon. He had me hooked.

"Uh oh! Here it comes again!" a male college student blurted from the row behind me, bursting into laughter.

This passage in the Bible was about a battle that King David, as an older, weaker man, experienced in Gath—the city of Goliath—where he and his men had to fight four of Goliath's sons, one of which was Ishbibenob. Last I remembered, this preacher had filled his sermon on this story with jokes and references to popular culture.

"My name is Ishbibenob!" the guest speaker proclaimed, pretending to hold out a sword. "You killed my father! Prepare to die!"

He's doing it again! I remembered a few of his jocular nuances from last time. Still, it was what I needed at the time. I put aside all my worries and let him drift me away into the world of David and Ishbibenob again.

"When David killed Goliath," the preacher said, "it was the first time he got *a head* of his competition!"

I joined the crowd in roaring hysterics; this man slew us with his corny jokes. I left that sermon ready to apply my positive mood to a lesson practice run that night. Once again, my lesson was saved from destruction.

CHAPTER 30

A Life-Changing Dream

I stood under the park pavilion, facing my eager audience. There were about fifty children, not the usual eight to twelve. There was no more time to practice. All that was left for me to do was open my mouth and speak.

As I unloaded my take on the stories of Enoch and Noah, every child's eyes locked on to mine. Having maintained a captive audience, I knew how I had to end the lesson. I asked everyone to bow their heads and close their eyes. This was what many pastors and evangelists would do at the end of a church service to try to get people to accept the gospel.

"Is there anyone here who's not sure if you're going to heaven but would like to know?" I said. "Raise your hand."

I scanned the entire crowd. No one raised a hand. Just when I was about to terminate the invitation, one little hand slowly lifted. Her head soon followed, glaring into my eyes in sincerity—it was Amy.

"You can talk to Rachel." I pointed behind her.

The child turned to see Rachel standing behind the crowd, clutching her Bible. She quietly got up from her seat and marched toward Rachel.

My eyes opened; I was lying on my side in bed. "3:30 a.m." faded into view from my alarm clock. I was now in the real world.

"Divine appointments—will you see them when they come . . . and, when they come . . . will you be ready to take them on?"

Those words, preached to me sixteen years ago, echoed in my mind that moment. What seemed like reality moments ago was but a figment of my imagination, but it seemed more real than many of my past dreams. What I had experienced before my eyes opened had opened my eyes to what could soon be reality. At this point, all I wanted to do was pray.

My knees hit the floor. My face plopped onto my bed.

"God, I don't know if that was just a dream," I prayed, "but it seemed so real! If there's any reason for me to have a dream like this, I'd like to claim this as a promise of what's to come."

I crawled back into bed. A surge of warmth and comfort overtook me as I drifted back into dreamland moments later.

CHAPTER 31

The Candy Man Can

I sat there at work that Thursday morning, September 26, 2013, pondering the Bible lesson I would be presenting in two days. All I could think about was a way to ensure that the children would have my undivided attention like how they were in my dream. I hashed out plans in my mind during work until a light-bulb moment struck.

"Children like candy, right?"

It wasn't a well-lit light bulb because I wasn't thinking straight. All I knew was that candy would be the legal tender on which to purchase attention from children. With candy dangling over their heads, the children would pay attention! They would have to *earn* that candy! They would need to be *quizzed* for that candy! It was a genius idea, at least for me at the time.

That evening, I pranced along the candy isles at Walmart. Two bags of Hershey's Miniatures caught me off guard. I slammed them into my cart, bought a few groceries, and raced back to my apartment.

First, one of the plastic Walmart bags quickly became the catalyst for all the Hershey's Miniatures. Next, I gave my computer keyboard another workout—devising a twenty-one-question quiz.

"They'll pay attention now. Yes, they will!" I clasped my hands in delight. "This was the best idea ever!"

Was it really?

CHAPTER 32

The Day of Reckoning

B *eep, beep, beep** Was I experiencing déjà vu? There was my alarm clock waking me up again at 7:00 a.m. on Saturday. It was September 28, 2013—the day of reckoning. I laughed, pondering the deep sleep that had overtaken me that night. Unlike last Saturday, I flicked off the alarm and leapt out of bed.

Snatching up the posters, I began another practice round as many times before. It began well. My words were clear, but I still tended to drift into monotone as I told the story.

I paused, staring at the notes I had taped to the backs of the posters. That moment, I had an epiphany over my final barrier to success. Those words that were supposed to guide me were what were killing my delivery.

"John, where's your faith?" I said.

Within a minute, those strips of taped words were off the posters and found a new home in the trash can. The tyranny was over! I was finally free to speak from the heart! After three successful practice rounds, I headed to Wayne's house. After gaining his approval to include candy and a quiz, we packed up the supplies and were on our way to the park.

Most of the ride that morning was dead silence. I sat in Wayne's car, staring at the passing trees. Strangely enough, no one uttered a word—not even the two new men riding in back. I couldn't dare break the silence; my mind was laser focused on my Bible lesson—on Amy.

Having arrived at the park, I swept the pavilion at record speed, then darted to the field for my final practice runs. The rest of the men and boys were playing football. I had joined them in the fun the past few times, but not now. I was in my own world.

"Mr. John!" a boy shouted from the other end of the field. "Come play football with us!"

"Mr. John!" he shouted minutes later, beckoning me from a huddle.

Wayne glanced my direction. I waved back and then pointed at my visuals.

"Let Mr. John alone!" he said. "He's practicing his Bible lesson!"

"Amy's getting saved today!" I muttered to myself every other sentence. I was certain of it.

Before I knew it, 11:00 a.m. hit. Wayne made the announcement—time to gather under the pavilion for the main events. Those were my final three rehearsals ever—no turning back. Next time, it was for real.

Taking a seat on the concrete floor, I peered around at the crowd; it resembled that of my dream—about fifty people. Children and adults filled every space on the benches—a lot of whom I'd never seen before. All extra folding chairs were occupied. Some people even sat on the concrete floor.

Perhaps Noah's ark was making a comeback and, this time, more than eight people were onboard. I'd never seen an audience this size at Bible Club. Surely they weren't here just to rock the boat, or, more accurately, rock the ark. I was both nervous and delighted. Failure wasn't an option today!

Rachel led the congregation in three songs. Wayne then oversaw the memory verse erasing game. It was on Gen 6:8—"But Noah found grace in the eyes of the LORD." The shorter nature of the verse made the game much quicker. My time was approaching rapidly. My heart raced.

"OK, everyone," Wayne said. "Today, we're doing something special. Mr. John brought some candy and is gonna quiz you over his lesson. If you all pay close attention you may be able to win some." He looked into my eyes. "OK, John . . . when you're ready."

I stood up, beckoning one of the men to follow me on stage. I handed him the posters to hold for me. I turned to face the crowd. It was bigger than I'd realized. The crowd locked their eyes onto me.

Was this moment really happening? My notes were gone; I left them back home in my trash can. There was no turning back! I had to act on faith. The stage was now mine to command.

My life flashed before my eyes—the past sixteen years from the "divine appointments" sermon until now—sixteen years of winding paths keeping me there for that moment. Could a "divine appointment" really be unfolding before my eyes? I swallowed my nerves, opened my mouth, and began to speak.

CHAPTER 33

It's Story Time

Although I taught this lesson many years ago, I was able to recall most of what I had said that day, probably because of all of my practice sessions and the emotions I had. I began my lesson with the following reminder and transition:

> Two lessons ago, we discussed Adam and Eve in the Garden of Eden—how the serpent tempted Eve into eating the forbidden fruit and she asked him to eat it as well, causing God to kick them out of the garden. Last lesson, we talked about Cain and Abel—the first two sons of Adam and Eve—how Cain killed his brother Abel, resulting in the first murder in history.

My words became solemn. My tone expressed gloom and sorrow:

> Now, we fast forward another seven hundred years. . . . God looks over the world . . . and all he sees . . . is wickedness.

That moment, Amy's countenance fell; she wasn't smiling anymore. Her face matched mine in the melodramatic. I continued:

God said, "I am so . . . sick . . . of the wickedness . . . of this world. Every thought in man's heart . . . is only evil . . . continually. Is there even one person who loves me?"

I believe that God knows everything. In my lesson, I was personifying the Godhead more for dramatic and relatable effect to my young audience. I began looking around the crowd, pretending to search for a "righteous" individual as I continued:

God looks around and he finds a guy named Enoch.

For clarity, the lesson package contained both the Enoch lesson and the Noah lesson with their visuals. Within it were two cards: one with the name "Enoch" on it and the other with the name "Methuselah" on it. Figuring I could utilize everything in the pack, I held up the card with "Enoch" on it and had my audience shout the name two or three times to let it sink into their heads. Returning to a melodramatic tone, I continued:

God spoke to Enoch and said, "Enoch, I'm sick of the wickedness of this world. Every thought in man's heart is only evil continually. I want to share my heart with you. I'm going to destroy this world. Right now, I'm not going to tell you how or when, but I'm going . . . to destroy . . . this world."

At that moment, all eyes glued to mine. They were ready for more. I continued:

"*Destroy the world?*" Enoch asked. "God, is there *any way* that we can *still* your *hand?*" God said, "Go around and preach that everyone needs to repent and turn to me, and, if they will repent, I may still my hand."

Of course, these conversations are not in the Bible. I was taking "artistic liberties" for dramatic effect. I began pacing around the stage, pretending to be Enoch on a mission as I continued:

So, Enoch would spend his time going around and shouting, "Repent! Repent! God is going to destroy this world! Repent and turn back to God!" But no one would repent. Enoch kept shouting, "Repent!," but everyone just laughed at him. They said, "God's not going to destroy the world! We're just fine! God probably doesn't even exist!"

I slowed down, developed a serene smile, and softly continued:

One day, Enoch's wife gave birth to a baby boy. Once again, God came to Enoch and said, "Enoch?" Enoch answered, "Here am I, Lord." God said, "Remember when I told you that I was going to destroy the world and that I told you that I wasn't going to tell you how or when? Well, now I'm going to tell you when, but I'm not going to tell you how."

I pointed sternly at the audience and shouted:

So, God points to Enoch's baby and says, "When *he dies* . . . judgment comes!"

The eyes of everyone in the audience bugged out; their attention intensified. I toned down my voice once again and continued:

So, Enoch named his boy Methuselah.

Holding out the card with the name "Methuselah" on it, I had the audience shout it out two or three times. Keep in mind that I was going to quiz them on this stuff. Returning to my calm cadence, I continued:

Methuselah means "When he dies judgment comes." Now, for several hundred years, Enoch continued to preach repentance, but the people wouldn't repent. Enoch took extra care of his son Methuselah because he knew that judgment would come after his son died. Because of this, Methuselah probably had the best health-care system known to man!

That last statement got a good chuckle from the crowd as I continued:

After a while, Enoch's constant preaching and caring for his son must have overwhelmed him. God decided to relieve Enoch of his burden by taking him to heaven. Now, God didn't kill Enoch. God just took him to heaven.

The children in the crowd perked in curiosity of what it meant for God to "take" Enoch to heaven. I continued with my "genius" exposition:

Now, the Bible has a very interesting way of describing this. It says, "Enoch walked with God and he was not for God took him." One moment Enoch was there. The next moment he was . . . not.

Everyone smiled—pondering. I left them hanging and continued:

Now, Enoch's son Methuselah lived a long time. In fact, Methuselah actually lived longer than anyone else on earth. He lived 969 years. That shows how long-suffering God is. God promised to destroy the world when Methuselah died and God let him live longer than anyone else in history.

Suddenly, the oldest boy—in his mid-teens—raised his hand.

"Mr. John," he proudly bellowed. "Wouldn't Enoch be the longest living person on the earth, seeing how he never died?"

"That's a good point," I said.

"Very good point." Rachel added. "That's quite an insightful question."

"Very clever question," I said, "but I was talking about the person who lived the longest . . . on *earth*."

Satisfied with the prolonged attention, I switched from Enoch and began talking about Noah:

About four hundred years later, God appeared to a man named Noah—the grandson of Methuselah and the great grandson of Enoch. God said, "Noah, I want to share my heart with you. Remember when I told Enoch that I was going to destroy the world and that I was going to tell him *when* but not *how*? Well, I'm going to tell *you* how. I'm going to destroy the world with a flood. Rain is going to fall from the sky and water is going to burst from the ground to cover the earth."

So, Noah said, "What do you want me to do, LORD?"

God replied, "I want you to build an ark. It's to be made of gopher wood. You're to cover it with pitch," which is probably a tar made out of tree sap. "It's going to be three hundred cubits long, fifty cubits wide, and thirty cubits tall."

I held up my forearm, pointed to it, and further explained:

A cubit is the distance from the elbow to the fingertips. Noah's was probably at least twenty-one inches long.

God said to Noah, "It's to have one window all around for ventilation and only one door. It's to have three floors."

Noah and his family—his wife, his three sons, and their wives—eight total people—spent about seventy-five to one hundred and twenty years building that ark. I could imagine how the people around him reacted when they saw Noah building that ark. Every day, he probably heard comments like "Hey, Noah! *Why* are you *building* that *ark*?" and Noah could have replied, "Because God's going to destroy the world with a flood! It is going to rain on the earth! God commanded me to build it! Repent before it is too late!"

Amy's face grew more concerned for the people in my story. I continued my fabricated conversation:

Noah could have even asked the people to help him build the ark and then the people could have responded with "You're crazy, Noah! It has never rained on the earth! There's no reason to repent. You're wasting your time! Why not join us for a party instead?"

Noah could have said, "Sorry, but I must obey God and keep building this ark."

After the ark was finally built, God said to Noah, "Go gather seven pairs of every kind of clean land animal and one pair of every kind of unclean land animal and bring them to the ark."

I can only imagine the mockery Noah received while doing this.

"Hey, Noah! What're you *doing*? Are you trying to start your own *zoo*?"

My last statement earned another good chuckle from the audience as I continued:

Noah could have replied, "No. God commanded me to bring these animals to the ark. God's going to flood the world, but these animals will be saved."

The people could have said, "You're crazy, Noah! It'll never rain!"

After Noah gathered all the animals to the ark, God did something . . . interesting. God caused all the animals to pair up and march into the ark. I can imagine the mockery that the people had when they saw that: "Hey, Noah! Nice trick! Can you teach them to *fetch, play dead*, or *roll over*?"

I was on a role with the campiness in such a serious story. The chuckling increased. Amy, on the other hand, retained a face of concern—captivated by the story. I continued:

After all the animals got into the ark, God commanded Noah and his family to enter. After Noah and his family got into the ark, the Bible says something . . . interesting. It says, "And *God* shut the door."

Suddenly, I began to lecture in a serious tone with a sudden glimmer of cleverness:

And, folks . . . when *God* . . . shuts . . . a door . . . only *God* . . . can *open* that door.

As several adults grunted in agreement, I felt proud of the profound "dogma" I had just spewed. A moment later, I felt awkward because I knew that such a statement wasn't directly from the Bible. Needless to say, it wasn't at all blasphemous nor did it merit any scowls from the audience. If God doesn't want a door to be open, there's no way anyone could force it open against his will.

The concept was still biblical to my knowledge. I cleared my throat and continued:

> For seven days . . . nothing happened. Noah and his family just stayed in the ark . . . and waited. I could only imagine the mockery from the people: "Hey, Noah! What are you all *doing* in there? Are you just going to live in there for the *rest of your lives* with all of those *animals?*"

At this point, I instructed my assistant to flip to the next poster. It was a rendition of Noah's ark with people surrounding it and laughing at it. I pointed at a boy in the picture and commented:

> On this picture, the artist rendered some little boy throwing a rock at the ark to illustrate how people mocked Noah and his family.

Turning back to face the audience, I continued:

> After seven days, the people noticed a gentle sprinkling from the sky.
> "It's rain!" the crowd exclaimed. "Let's hope it doesn't get any worse!"
> Sooner or later, the sprinkling turned into a harsh downpour. The people began to panic.

I increased the speed of my words and the intensity of my voice nearing the climax of the story:

> They ran up to the door, banged their fists on it, and screamed, "Noah! Noah! We believe you now! The rain is coming! Please, let us in!"
> Noah replied, "I can't! I'm sorry! God shut the door! I can't open it!"
> They screamed louder, "*Please,* Noah! We're going to *die!*"
> Noah replied, "I'm sorry! . . . *You had your chance!*"
> The people ran to look for something to climb onto. All of a sudden, the ground cracked open next to them and water gushed up into the air! Whoosh!
> "Whoa!" The people screamed!
> They rushed to the trees and climbed them to the top. After the water level caught up to them, they swam

with all their might to the mountains and climbed up to the tops. Soon, the water reached over the mountains.

Swimming to the point of exhaustion, they reached the ark and screamed, "Please, Noah! Let us in! We're going to drown!"

Noah replied, "I'm sorry! I can't! God shut the door! Only God can open the door! I warned you! *You had your chance!*"

Every eye was glued to me that moment as I dropped the climactic tone and switched to a more calm and serene mood:

As the water level continued to rise . . . the screams continued, but they eventually got quieter . . . and quieter . . . and quieter until, finally, they stopped . . . and all that was left on the earth . . . was water . . . and Noah's ark.

That moment, I paused to examine the audience. The adults were wiping away tears. The children were staring at me, jaws hanging. I had never seen such a response from the audience at Bible Club before. I calmly continued:

For forty days . . . it rained—forty days of constant downpour as Noah and his family waited . . . thinking about all the screams they had heard from the people that had drown.

After forty days, Noah looked out the window to notice the rain had stopped. He knew it would take a while for the water to sink down and for the ground to dry up enough for them to be able to exit the ark. Noah and his family stayed in the ark after the rain stopped for about four months.

Noah then decided to release a raven out the window to see if it could bring back signs of life. The raven eventually landed on a corpse floating out of the water.

Noah was probably like, "OooooK? That didn't quite work out like I had expected."

Once again, I had earned a slight chuckle from the crowd for that last statement. I continued:

A while later, Noah released a dove. The dove later returned to him with an olive branch in its beak. Noah realized that it was safe to exit the ark.

God opened the door and let Noah and his family out of the ark. To honor God for protecting him and his family from destruction, Noah built an altar and sacrificed some of the extra clean animals on it. God smelled a sweet savor from the smoke of the burnt offering.

With dramatic awe on my face, I peered up toward the sky and continued:

Noah looked up into the sky . . . and saw . . . the most beautiful rainbow that had ever existed—the very *first* rainbow that had ever existed.

Rachel smiled, obviously picturing the rainbow in her mind. I continued, adding serenity to my voice:

God said, "I put this rainbow in the sky as a covenant to you . . . that I will never . . . destroy the world with a flood . . . ever again."

With the audience still captivated, my emotions began to rise. My opportunity to evangelize was unfolding. It was now or never. I had to get it out!

CHAPTER 34

It's Time to Preach

I did it! I was finally done . . . at least with the story portion of my lesson. I could finally relieve my mind from recalling all of those pesky details that I had strived to retain in my rehearsals. With a captive audience and a purpose in my heart to drive it home with a bang, I built up a stern voice and continued:

> Now, folks, this story is very important for us, because it shows that God hates sin. He created this world and he has a right to judge it. We are *not* just wasting our time here telling you these stories.

Suddenly, I began to preach:

> These stories that we tell you here at Bible Club . . . they are *not* just *stories!* They are *real!* And God put them in the Bible for a *reason!* He *wants* us to know the *truth!*

Pointing at the poster visual depicting Noah's ark, I continued my rant:

> Did you *know* that the Bible *predicted* that people would not believe *this story?* In fact, it predicted *why* they wouldn't believe! In 2 Pet 3, it says, "Knowing *this* . . .

there shall come in the last days . . . *scoffers* . . . walking
after their own lust!"

That moment, I feared that the audience would be taken
aback by my unexpected morph into "pulpit mode." This wasn't
the usual demeanor for lessons at Bible Club. Surprisingly, the
children seemed fine with it—eyes still fixed to mine. The adults
actually seemed to be enjoying it.

Glancing back at Amy, I noticed that her face expressed deep
sorrow for the "scoffers" to which I was alluding. Everything was
going great so far. There was no turning back at this point. I had
to keep going!

> Scoffers are people who *mock* the *Bible*! They don't want
> to believe that it's true, because they don't want to believe
> that God *exists* and that he has a *right* to *judge* the *world*!
> ". . . walking after their own lust"—These people's
> whole lives are governed by whatever pleases their own
> flesh.
> ". . . and saying, 'Where is the promise of His com-
> ing? For since the fathers fell asleep, all things continue
> as they were from the beginning of creation.'"

At this moment, my voice echoed over the horizons. I can't
remember ever shouting louder in my life than I did with my following words:

> "For *this* cause, they *willingly are ignorant*!'"

I toned it down and continued:

> What are they ignorant *of*? . . . That there was a flood.
> What it actually says is that the earth stood *out* of the
> water . . . and *in* the water.

Staring intently at the audience, I shouted:

> *Remember the fountains of the great deep* that I had men-
> tioned earlier? . . . *Whoosh!*

The children nodded in agreement—mouths hanging wide
open as I continued:

"...and that the *earth*...being *overflowed* with water...
perished!" But they don't *want* to believe *that*.

I began mocking arrogantly:

They say, "*All* things...*continue* as they *were*...*from* the
beginning of *creation!*"

Looking to the sky, I erupted in anger:

Even though the earth looks like it *used* to be under
water and there are *millions* of *dead things* buried and
contorted all over the place under the ground! They say,
"*All* things *continue* as they *were*...*from* the beginning
of *creation!*"

I lifted my finger skyward over the audience and shouted as
loudly as I could:

They are *willingly*...*ignorant!*

I sighed and calmed down to a quieter tone:

The passage goes on to say...that the earth is being reserved unto fire...for the perdition...of ungodly men.

That moment, I placed my hands behind my back and began
pacing around as I continued:

Judgment is coming, folks....Judgment...is coming
...but it's not going to be by water. It's going to be by fire.

Suddenly, my emotions flared up once again. I began swinging my finger at the crowd while lifting my voice over the horizons
once again:

But *you*...*don't*...*have*...to *be*...*judged!*...*You*...
can...*believe!* That simple *faith*...that *Enoch* had...
and that simple *faith*...that *Noah* had—that *simple faith*
in *God—saved them!*

My arms began to animate wildly as I continued shouting:

When everyone else *died, they were saved!* And that same *faith* that *Enoch* had . . . and that same *faith* that *Noah* had . . . *you can have!*

I began swinging my finger aggressively over the audience's heads:

You can believe! . . . Even if *everyone else* . . . in the *whole world* . . . doesn't believe . . . *you can!* . . . *You can!* . . . *You* . . . *can* . . . *believe!* And, folks, when you believe in God, not only are you not judged, but you . . . can live . . . with God . . . in heaven . . . *forever!* *That* . . . is the greatest . . . thing . . . in the *whole* . . . *world!*

At this point, my energy and preaching demeanor wore out. I calmly continued:

Can we pray now? Can everyone bow your heads and close your eyes . . . and pray with me?

I wasn't sure what I was doing at this point. I had just turned a Bible lesson about Enoch and Noah into some kind of evangelistic invitation, yet I had never mentioned Jesus or the gospel. I had to make this work somehow. I began praying out loud:

If there's anyone here today who would say, "I'm not sure if I know that I'm going to heaven when I die," could you just pray with me?

Dear God, I know that I'm a sinner. I know that, because of my sin, I don't deserve to go to heaven. I deserve to be *judged!* God, I'm not *worthy* of you. Oh God, help me! I want to be *saved!* You sent Jesus down to earth to live a perfect life and to die on the cross to pay for our sins and I believe that. Oh, God, I *believe that!* I don't *want* to be *judged!* I want you to *save me!* I want to live with you in heaven forever! I want you to love me! I want to love you! I accept your free gift of salvation. Amen.

Having finished the prayer and observing everyone's eyes open, I had to clarify my actions:

> Now, folks . . . if you just prayed that prayer with me . . .
> and you *meant* it . . . then *you* . . . are . . . *saved* . . . and *you*
> . . . are *going* . . . to *heaven*!

Putting my hands behind my back, I began pacing slowly across the audience with a smile:

> *Jesus* said . . . "My sheep . . . hear my voice . . . and I know
> them . . . and they follow me . . . and I . . . give . . . to them
> . . . eternal . . . *life* . . . and they . . . will *never* perish."

Suddenly, I regained a boost of energy. I looked up to the sky, waved my finger, and preached:

> "*Neither* shall *any* man *pluck* them out of my *hand*!"

I began stomping my foot and pounding my fist into my palm:

> Folks, when *you are saved* . . . it . . . is . . . *sealed*!

Opening my hand toward the audience and slowly clenching it into a grasp, I softly pleaded:

> God . . . has . . . you . . . in . . . his . . . *hand* . . . and *you* . . .
> are *going* to *heaven*.

I lifted my finger to the sky and began preaching loudly again:

> And *no one* . . . can *ever* . . . take . . . that . . . *away from*
> *you*!

I was drained that moment—reduced to a serene calm. Placing my hands behind my back, I paced back away from the audience to their left:

> Our memory verse today says, "But Noah . . . found *grace*
> . . . in the eyes . . . of the LORD."

I regained one last surge of emotion, thrust my finger toward the audience, and preached my final plea:

> Will *you* . . . find *grace* . . . in the eyes . . . of the Lord?

It was over. I'd been speaking for over forty-five minutes. All I could do was perform a slight bow to the audience then return to my seat on the concrete floor. To my surprise, the crowd followed with a standing ovation and cheers as I looked down at the floor.

CHAPTER 35

The Quiz

There I sat on the concrete—in disbelief of what had just transpired. All the pressures and anxiety of the past few weeks were gone—all but one more concern—what was Amy going to do about it? Never had I been more satisfied with one of my public speeches, but would it actually accomplish anything? I had to find out!

"All right, Mr. John now has a special treat for everyone." Wayne stood up—hands clasped together. "He's going to quiz you on his lesson. If you answer any questions correctly you get a piece of candy."

I marched to the table to retrieve my quiz sheet and bag of Hershey's Miniatures, and then turned to face the audience. All of the children had smiles on their faces, eager to win those sweet treats—all except one—Amy. Her eyes were lost in mine. The look of conviction and concern on her face was a Kodak moment. She had the appearance of someone who'd just been put through a crisis—looking to me as the one who'll give her the answer to life, the universe, and everything.

What was I doing here with a *quiz* and a *bag of candy*? Those children were licking their lips, but Amy could care less about the chocolate! All she wanted was to talk to me, but I was holding her back! This was extremely awkward! I'd dug myself into a pit and had to climb out.

"All right," I said, clearing my throat, "there are twenty-one questions on this quiz. That should give many a chance to win some candy. Afterward, we'll divvy out the leftovers. Question number one: 'Who was the man that God took into heaven?'"

"Enoch!" a little girl shouted, running up eagerly to snag a piece of chocolate.

"Question number two," I continued. "'Who was Enoch's son?'"

"Ooo! Ooo! I remember!" a little boy shouted. "Methuselah!"

As the boy ran up to get a treat, I glanced back at Amy. Her face hadn't changed. This had to be torture for her. The situation was simultaneously hilarious and sad. As much as I wanted to reach out to her, all I could do was continue the quiz.

"'Who built the ark?' . . . 'How many floors were in the ark?' . . . 'How many doors were on the ark?' . . . 'How many windows were on the ark?'"—I paced myself through each question, trying to finish as soon as possible. Amy's eyes were still locked on to mine, not the candy. She never wanted any and never participated in the quiz. She just wanted to talk.

CHAPTER 36

The Confrontation

T he quiz was finally over! I put the bag back onto the table, then beckoned Wayne to distribute the leftovers. As the children darted up to satisfy their sweet tooth, I stepped off to the side and waited. Without hesitation, Amy approached.

"Um, Mr. John?" she said. "Thank you for that Bible lesson. It really inspired me. The words you said, the way you said them, and those visuals you used really inspired me. . . . You got *my* attention."

It was my perfect chance to shine! She was locked in and thirsting for it. All of the hard work was over. All I needed to do was hand the gospel to her on a silver platter. This should be a slam dunk for me, right?

"Thank you." It was all I could muster for some reason.

"Were you nervous?" Amy prodded with a large grin. "I think I could tell. I thought you looked nervous when you were speaking, but you still did a great job. You seem like you can overcome your nervousness very well."

"Thank you." I chuckled. "I'm always nervous whenever I speak in public. I mean, I love to speak, but . . . I don't think I'm very good at it. Usually, I can overcome my nerves by walking around on the stage. It helps me think clearly and makes my transitions better." I mocked some of the pacing I did during my lesson.

"Well," Amy said, "I just wanted to thank you for the lesson and tell you that it really inspired me."

"Thank you," I blurted once again.

We stood there staring at each other for a moment. *Why couldn't I share the gospel with her?* This was the perfect opportunity, but no words could come out!

"So, Mr. John," said Amy, ". . . what do you do for a living?"

"Oh, I'm a software developer at PCC."

"Oh, really? That's cool. Do you live in an apartment?"

"Yes. I live in an apartment about five minutes from the campus."

"That's cool. We live with our mom in an apartment. Recently, we've seen a couple roaches. I think we have a roach problem now."

"Aw, that's too bad," I sympathized.

"Yeah, hopefully we can get an exterminator soon."

Once again, we stared at each other. I knew what I really wanted to say and could sense that Amy wanted to hear it.

"Hey, Mr. John," her sister Holly said from behind. "Would you like to play the jump rope game?"

"Uh . . . sure," I said reluctantly.

I grabbed an end of the rope as one of the adult ladies' mothers, who was visiting that day, grabbed the other end. Amy, Holly, and a few other children began jumping while singing a song. All hope of sharing the gospel with Amy was slipping away. Would I be stuck holding the rope until everyone left? Something had to happen and it had to happen fast!

A couple of minutes later, Wayne ignorantly saved the day with a hilariously unexpected request.

"Hey, John, one of the boys needs to use the bathroom, but there's no bathroom in the park. I'm giving some of us a ride to the local Home Depot. Would you like to come?"

"Sure!" I cheered, dropping my end of the rope. "Sorry, everyone, but I'm going with Wayne and some others to the Home Depot for a restroom break. Anyone else need to go?"

"No," the others playing the jump rope game answered.

Somehow, I knew that this boy's unexpected call to nature would be part of this so-called "divine appointment," but I wasn't sure how. After all, in my dream, Rachel was the one who talked to Amy about the gospel. Perhaps my part was done and I just had to be removed from the picture to let Rachel do her part.

Although over half of the children and adults piled into cars to go to the Home Depot, Rachel and Amy were of the few that remained. That was something blatantly apparent to me at the moment.

CHAPTER 37

The Call to Nature

I sat in silence, watching the trees pass from Wayne's car window on that ride to the Home Depot. During the whole trip, I fantasized a hypothetical conversation between Rachel and Amy. If a conversation never took place, perhaps Amy would still be at the park when we all returned. Maybe, by then, I'd be able to conjure the words for her.

After arriving at Home Depot, everyone lined up for the restrooms—the children first followed by the adults. As I awaited my turn, one of the adult ladies in line confronted me.

"Wow, John, your Bible lesson was amazing!"

"Thank you." I sheepishly grinned. "I was hoping to get the gospel out somehow in case any of the children needed to hear it."

"Well, you certainly touched a lot of people. The way you spoke with such emotion was really moving."

"Thanks."

While the majority of us were at the Home Depot ready to answer nature's call, something special was brewing back at the park . . .

CHAPTER 38

The Conversion

While most of us were waiting in line to answer nature's call, Amy and Rachel remained at the park together. Apparently, Amy couldn't get my Bible lesson out of her head and had to talk to someone about it. The jump rope game was no longer vying for her attention.

"Hello, Miss Rachel." Amy shyly approached.

"Oh, hi, Amy. How are you?" said Rachel.

"I'm fine," said Amy. "You know . . . Mr. John's lesson really inspired me."

"Oh, *really*? In what way did it *inspire* you?"

"Well . . . it really makes me happy. I mean . . . it's really sad that all those people had to die, but . . . what makes me happy is that . . . all they had to do was *believe* and they could've been *saved*."

The gears began turning in Rachel's head. "*Wow! She actually caught on to that!*" she thought.

"So, Amy," Rachel said, "do you know if you're going to heaven after you die?"

"I don't think *anyone* can *really* know for *sure*."

"Huh, well, *I* do," Rachel bellowed in playful mockery. "Would you like me to show you how you can know for sure?"

"OK."

Rachel got out her Bible and walked the child through various passages from the Bible including some from the Romans Road—Rom 3:23, Rom 6:23, Rom 5:8, and Rom 10:9–13. After discussing points from the Bible lesson, Amy indicated that she wanted to live with Jesus in heaven and didn't want to be like the people who, according to the way I told the story, banged on the door of Noah's ark and couldn't get in.

Amy prayed a prayer, asking Jesus to save her from her sins and to live with him in heaven. Upon concluding the prayer, she jumped to her feet.

"I've got to tell my sister what I just did!" she said.

Holly was out in the field playing a game with the other remaining children. Amy ran out to her to explain what had just transpired. Afterward, she ran to each of the adults she could find and hugged them.

"Mr. John's Bible lesson really inspired me," she said, "and I just got *saved* today!"

CHAPTER 39

The Good News

I'd just finished my "divine appointment" with the Home Depot restroom, blissfully ignorant of what had transpired back at the park. I continued to pray for Amy and Rachel to talk as I waited for the rest of my comrades to finish freshening up.

Upon returning to the park, we found it almost deserted. Most of the Bible Club supplies were already packed. All that remained were Rachel and another lady standing under the pavilion; the biggest grin was plastered on Rachel's face—her eyes were locked on to mine.

"John, you're never gonna guess what just happened while you were gone!"

Rachel relayed to me her story with Amy. It was as if I was experiencing déjà vu.

"Whenever I lead a child to pray," she said, "I usually take their reactions with a grain of salt, because it's hard to tell if they're really sincere and if they really understand what they're doing. But, as soon as we said 'Amen,' she jumped to her feet, smiled at me, and said, 'I've got to tell my sister what I just did!'"

She described to me how Amy ran out to tell Holly and then hugged all the adults and told them as well.

"I remember several times talking to her about the gospel," said Rachel, "but she just didn't quite get it. Whatever you said in your lesson somehow must have been what was needed to soften her heart to make her susceptible to it." Rachel's excitement and smile built up once again. "Wow! Did you expect anything like *that* to happen?"

"Somehow, I knew you were gonna tell me this," I said, and then expounded to her the dream I had the previous Wednesday night.

"Wow! I guess you got a vision of the future from the Lord."

"I really don't know."

Wayne, Rachel, and I packed the remaining Bible Club supplies into Wayne's car—the three of us in silence—shocked by what had transpired with Amy. My only dilemma was that I'd have to wait an entire week to talk to Amy post-conversion. Next time I see her, would she still have the gospel on her mind?

For the first five minutes of the drive back to PCC, none of us in the car spoke a word; we remained in shock. Suddenly, Wayne gathered the courage to break the silence.

"Well . . . it seems like the Holy Spirit really used you mightily today."

"Yeah, thanks," I mumbled.

We sat in awkward silence for another minute. I decided to break it once again with an inside joke Wayne and I had shared the last few weeks—talking like New York gangsters.

"I guess da Holy Spirit helped intraduce ha to da Lawd," I mocked.

"Yeah, yeah," Wayne mocked back with a similar accent.

We continued our gangster charade about our usual joke about baseball bats as gangsters' "little friends" (weapons) with our fake accents until we arrived at the campus parking lot.

"See you, John." Wayne waved as I walked to my van. "Thanks for coming today and good job on the lesson."

"Yup. Thanks."

I hopped into my van and returned to my apartment. Beginning my ritualistic shower after Bible Club, I sat down in the tub, shaking uncontrollably as the hot water sprayed over me.

"I can't believe that just happened!" I repeated to myself over and over, rocking back and forth.

Truth is definitely stranger than fiction! I began comparing my dream to reality: both had me preach my Bible lesson and both had Rachel share the gospel with Amy, but reality was much more chaotic.

"*A restroom break at Home Depot? Are you kidding me?* Did it all boil down to some boy's '*call to nature?*'"

I laughed uncontrollably at all the chaos leading up to the so-called "divine appointment."

"There was no 'call to nature' in my *dream!*" I said to myself, "*That's what ultimately leads to Rachel and Amy discussing the gospel?* Utterly hilarious!"

CHAPTER 40

A Hearty Congratulation

"So, Evangelist John Mynyk, huh?" my friend Alan (who is now deceased, may he rest in glory) greeted me from his mobile chair—Rachel proudly standing beside him. It was about noon after the Sunday morning church service at PCC, September 29, 2013.

"Oh." I chuckled. "I take it Rachel told you about what happened in Bible Club."

"Yeah," he said. "I heard that you were . . . quite the preacher there."

"Yeah," said Rachel. "You sounded just like an old-time evangelist!"

"I guess if that's what it sounded like." I laughed. "I was like walking around in the pavilion waving my arms and shouting, 'Even if everyone else in the whole world doesn't believe, you can!' I wasn't really planning to start preaching toward the end like that, but . . . I don't know . . . I think I just got a little carried away."

"It was *absolutely amazing*!" Rachel said, staring at me with a plastered grin.

"Really? Just remember that you're the one who led Amy to the Lord."

"We *both* had a part in leading her to the Lord."

CHAPTER 41

A Gift for the Convert

Monday morning, September 30, 2013, found me struggling to code at work. My mind was focused on one thing—Amy. I had to see her again. I had to know if she still believed the gospel.

Lunch had arrived, but I wasn't eating. Instead, I was invading the campus bookstore. This was a ritual of mine for at least a month; I was accomplishing two things during lunch—enriching my mind and shedding weight I had gained during my doctoral studies.

I picked up a book on Koine Greek and began rehearsing the alphabet, indirect articles, and basic conjugations. A quick glance to my right revealed a shelf of beautiful Bibles of various sizes, shapes, and colors.

"That's it! A Bible!" Another light bulb moment came to me. "I'll buy Amy a Bible! If she enjoys reading Rachel's, she'll enjoy reading her own!"

I searched the wall of Bibles looking for the perfect one for Amy. It had to be small enough to carry around, but contain print large enough to read without a magnifying glass. It wasn't long before I stumbled upon the optimal solution—a compact King James Bible. It met all criteria. It even had a unique color scheme—cyan and brown leather with an irregular splat medallion on the magnetic security flap—a nice complement to Amy's favorite outfit of the 1960s era.

That evening, I decided to write a personal message to Amy in the opening spread of the new Bible. After practicing typing out a message to get the exact wording, I carefully wrote on the inside cover the following:

> Amy,
>
> Thank you for listening to my lesson about Enoch and Noah. I am glad that you believe in Jesus.
>
> September 28, 2013 would be your spiritual birthday.
>
> I noticed that you seemed eager to read Rachel's Bible, so I thought I would get you one.
>
> Here are some key Bible passages for you:
> How to help someone get saved
> "The Romans Road"
> (Romans 3:23) "All have sinned"
> (Romans 6:23) "Sin brings death. God brings life"
> (Romans 5:8) "God loves us. Jesus died for us"
> (Romans 10:9–13) "Call on the name of the Lord to be saved"
>
> Prediction that people would not believe in the world-wide flood in the days of Noah (II Peter 3:3–7)

On the blank page after the inside cover, I wrote the following:

> Never let anyone discourage you from believing in God.
> I will not forget you.
> Your friend,
> John Mynyk

CHAPTER 42

Patience Is a Virtue

"*Where's Amy?* I thought she'd be here!" I stood under the pavilion, sweeping. My gift lay on the table. Saturday, October 5, 2013, couldn't have arrived soon enough. I'd be the first person to greet Amy.

"Hello, Mr. John." It was one of the boys, huffing and running up to me.

"Why are you standing there?" he asked. "Would you like to come play football with us?"

"I guess," I mumbled. "Have you seen Amy and Holly? I really wanna give Amy this Bible for getting saved last week."

"Oh." The boy chuckled. "Amy and Holly are out of town this week. They should be back next week."

My heart sank to the floor. *I'd have to wait another week to see Amy?* My stay in Florida was growing short! I had to see her at least once before I left for Colorado!

"Oh." I sighed. "I really don't want anyone to steal this Bible. It has personal notes in it for Amy."

The boy stared at me for a moment, obviously growing impatient. "It should be fine. Just leave it on the table. Come play football with us, Mr. John."

Patience Is a Virtue

What else could I do? I had to block Amy from my mind and play some football.

CHAPTER 43

Spinning Around in Circles

It was Saturday, October 12—two weeks since I had seen Amy. For a certainty, she wouldn't be absent a second time, especially after her gospel experience. I was back under the pavilion—Bible in hand ready for her.

"Hello, Mr. John. What's that?" It wasn't Amy, but a precious little girl about six to eight years old.

"It's a gift for Amy for liking my Bible lesson and getting saved two weeks ago," I said.

"Wow. Can I look at it?"

"Sure," I said, handing it to her. "Just be careful not to hurt it. I want it in mint condition when I give it to her."

The child flipped through the pages, admiring the quality. "Um . . . Mr. John . . . can I have it?"

I burst out laughing; her question caught me off guard. "You want me to just . . . *give* this to you?"

"Uh . . . yeah," the girl said. Her heart-melting grin amused me.

"But what if Amy shows up?"

"Amy's out of town this week."

My heart skipped a beat. "*Out of town? Again?*"

"Yeah."

"How do you know? Did she tell you?"

"No. One of the other kids told me," she said. "He goes to the same school."

"Are you sure about that?"

"Yeah."

As I was about to surrender to total disgust, the child involuntarily cheered me up with an unexpected hilarious request.

"Spin me around, Mr. John!" she cheered, reaching her arms out to me. I'd never done that with a child before, but I'd seen some of the other adults fulfill her odd request to know what she meant. There's always a first time for everything.

Placing the Bible on the table, I gripped her wrists tightly and began spinning around, lifting her off the ground. Soon, she was in the air lying parallel to the floor and at eye level with me.

"Weeee!" She laughed, staring into my eyes. While spinning around, the girl nagged again, "Mr. John . . . are you sure I can't have that Bible?"

I laughed; her persistence was golden! "Yes," I chuckled, mockingly looking into her eyes.

"But Amy's out of town this week. I really want it."

"But it has personal notes for Amy inside it. It even has her name written in it."

"So?"

I brought her to a safe landing.

"I really want it," she said, "because . . . I don't have my own Bible."

"But Amy probably doesn't either," I said.

"Yes she does. She already has her own Bible. I don't have one. Could I just have it?" Her playful insistence on getting that Bible sent the cuteness factor off the charts.

"Are you sure Amy already has one?" I smiled, playing into her fabrication.

Brushing her shoe into the floor behind her, the child shyly glanced into my eyes. "I'm pretty sure she does."

"Somehow, I doubt that. You're probably just making that up."

The girl continued staring into my eyes. "Please, can I have it, Mr. John?"

"Sorry, but this Bible is for Amy. If you really need a Bible, I'll see if we can work something out, OK?"

"OK. Thank you, Mr. John."

As the child ran off to join her friends in a game on the field, Wayne approached. I expounded to him what had transpired. He assured me the girl didn't really know if Amy possessed her own Bible. Needless to say, her antics cheered me up enough to wait for another week for Amy to return.

CHAPTER 44

Third Time's a Charm

Saturday, October 19 found me under the pavilion once again—Bible in hand. It had been three weeks since I'd seen Amy. At this point, I wondered if something bad had happened to her. After all, I'd never seen her and Holly skip a Bible Club since they had first attended. Ten minutes of waiting revealed no children at all arriving to the park.

Suddenly, I caught something out of the corner of my eye; two familiar girls arrived from their car in their Woodstock outfits once again. I buried my emotions, gathered my dignity, and marched out to meet them.

"Hi, Amy," I said, clearing my throat.

"Hi, Mr. John," she replied, and then glanced at the table of Bible Club supplies under the pavilion.

Holly continued walking toward the field to meet other children who were beginning to arrive.

"I . . . I got you a gift," I stammered to Amy. I held out the Bible in its original box. "This is my thanks to you for liking my Bible lesson and getting saved."

The child curiously opened the box and glanced at the Bible for a moment. Giving me a quick hug, she then ran toward the pavilion. "Where is it?" she muttered, digging through the bag of songs.

"Whatcha looking for, Amy?"

"I'm looking for that 'I Believe the Bible' song," she said, religiously flipping through the books in the bag. "Come on. Where is it? . . . Ah ha! There it is!"

Pulling the familiar sheet music from the bag, she sat down on the bench under the pavilion and began staring at it.

"You . . . *like* that song?" I asked, sitting down next to her.

"Uh huh." She nodded, and then began singing it to me.

The song had a simple melody with six short verses—each verse consisting of a small sentence repeated three times followed by a clarifying sentence. The song's words explain the singer's belief in the Bible, belief in Jesus, acknowledgment of sin, acknowledgment of Jesus' death and resurrection, then end with an ask for others to receive him and be saved.

"Again!" she cheered, repeating the song.

"Again!" she exclaimed, repeating the song likewise.

I chuckled and joined her in singing it.

"Again!" she cheered, singing it for a fourth time.

"Again!" she shouted, having sung it to me five times.

"Is this your favorite song?" I laughed.

"Mmm hmm." She nodded.

Looking around aggressively, Amy's eyes locked on to Rachel who was standing nearby in the field. "Miss Rachel!" she cheered. Jumping to her feet, the girl darted to her friend, hugging her aggressively.

"Mr. John!" a boy shouted to me from behind.

Turning back, I noticed two familiar boys swinging on the swing set.

"Come play with us!" they said.

One of them tossed a tennis ball into my hands indicating that we'd continue the swing-set-tennis-ball ritual. I began to play their little game, but my mind was not with them. It was on Amy and Rachel. I attempted to eavesdrop on their conversation. Rachel began reading my notes in Amy's Bible to her. Having finished, they went silent. Turning back to them, I caught them both staring back at me—huge smiles.

"That's so sweet!" said Rachel.

Running up to me for another hug, Amy then returned to Rachel. They began reading together from Amy's new Bible. At that point, I was able to relax and focus on the tennis ball game.

CHAPTER 45

An End to a Contract

I t was Thursday, October 31, 2013—five days after my blessed reunion with Amy. My time in Florida was coming to an end. I pondered all of the winding paths of my life's ambitions over the past fifteen years in Florida with the "divine appointment" as its climax. Those past three months of my work contract extension were the most amazing months in my life. Alas, my work contract and stay in Florida were coming to a close.

Today was the last day of my staff contract. After that, I probably wouldn't set foot on PCC's campus for a while. I still had two weeks left before my apartment lease ended, but I could afford such a vacation now, thanks to the contract extension. I was still planning to attend Bible Club the next two Saturdays.

At the end of my work shift, I marched into the IT manager's office to announce my departure. At this time, Mr. Tyler had retired about a month prior, leaving the position for a temporary overseer until it got officially filled.

"Well, this is it," I announced to the new man in the office. "Drumroll please."

The man chuckled, playing along with me.

Mimicking a drum sound with my mouth, I removed my work keys and staff ID card, placing them on his desk. Continuing the drumming sound, I pretended to rip invisible badges and stripes off my shirt and shoulders and placed them onto the desk.

"Well, that was interesting," I said. "I've officially been honorably discharged from active duty, sir. Wish me luck."

"Are you sure you know what you're doing?" the man asked. "We'd still be happy to take you back."

"Thanks for the offer. It's tempting, but . . . I guess I'm just gonna go out on a limb and see what's out there for me in Colorado."

"Well, we really appreciate your help all these years and wish you luck on your new endeavors."

CHAPTER 46

Goodbye Bible Club

November 2 and November 9 of 2013 were my final two Saturdays at Bible Club. After that, I'd be leaving the following Thursday morning. Although the first Saturday showed me nothing special, that final one was one I'll never forget.

My new ritual was to play the tennis-ball-swing-set game with the same two boys since the previous two Saturdays. As I lobbed the tennis ball at the swings, a commotion arose in the pavilion. I had to investigate. "Excuse me," I blurted, marching over to the group.

There stood Amy, clutching her new Bible to her heart. All the adults stood around her. "Yeah, please pray for me," she said. A concerned look grew on her face. "Please pray that I'll have the strength and courage to share the gospel with my friends and family."

"We definitely will," Rachel assured her.

My heart went out for the child in mixed feelings. From one aspect, I was proud of her beyond belief—almost ashamed that she could be much bolder with the gospel than I'd ever been. From another aspect, I felt sorry for her, wondering if an eight-year-old girl would end up taking on a spiritual battle alone with little guidance and discipleship.

I returned to the swing set game after the boys beckoned me. About fifteen minutes later, I heard a girl burst into tears. I looked out to the pavilion once again. To my surprise, it wasn't Amy. It was a little girl who was sitting on the bench next to Rachel. The girl was overcome in sorrow. She was the older sister of the little girl who had asked me for Amy's Bible a couple of weeks ago.

"I told her that today was Mr. John's last day at Bible Club," Rachel said to me, ". . . and she started crying."

I honestly don't remember if I'd ever talked to this girl before or if she even knew I existed. I smiled at Amy. Amy smiled back, and then stared compassionately at the weeping child.

"Why don't you go give Mr. John a hug?" Rachel said to the child.

The girl stumbled up to me while looking at the ground. Standing next to me for a moment, she looked up into my eyes, sniffled, and held out her arms. I met her embrace as she continued weeping.

"Don't leave us, Mr. John!" she cried. "Please don't!"

I was at a loss for words; there was nothing clever I could think of to say that could quell her concern. "It's OK," I whispered. "It's OK."

The emotional child glanced up into my eyes again—hugging me harder and bawling uncontrollably.

"It's OK," I repeated. "Maybe I could come back and visit sometime soon."

I walked with her back to Rachel. "Wow!" I gasped. "I wasn't expecting that. I didn't even think she knew me very well."

"I guess you don't realize how much you really care about someone until you find out they're leaving," Rachel said with a smile. "Hey, I know what!" she added. "Why don't we all make some *goodbye* cards for *Mr. John*?"

As I headed back to the swing set to continue the tennis ball ritual, all the girls sitting at the table under the pavilion began digging into construction paper. Soon, we were packed up for the day and had bid our farewells. As I rode in Wayne's car for the final time, I decided to read to the passengers each card the girls had made. Here's a description of some of the cards:

On the cover of the card from Amy was a drawing of two snowcapped mountains. It read:

For Mr. John From: Amy.

Inside it read:

John it was so fun having you here. You made us so happy and laugh and smile. You taught a good lesson for us. I will never forget you. Thank you for making us have a good time.

The card from the girl who got emotional about my leaving had nothing on the cover. Inside it read:

Dear Mr. John, I will miss you so much because you have been at Bible Club for so long. I will miss you in Colorado and you did not tell me that you were going to leave. I will miss you so much, so here is a letter for when you leave me. I started to cry because Bible Club is falling apart and I am getting sadder and sadder. It's just so sad to me. Please come back on the weekend. Please, Mr. John. I love you so much. Have fun in Colorado Mr. John. We all will miss you.

As I read all the cards, I wondered if I was doing the right thing by leaving. I sat there in silence, pondering all the wonderful people and the blessed memories I had shared with them for the last fifteen years in Florida. My emotions wanted me to stay to continue helping out in Bible Club and to disciple Amy, but my conscience assured me that it was time for me to move on.

CHAPTER 47

Moving On

About two weeks after having moved to Colorado, I was still thinking about Amy. As I was riding in Daniel's van to go grocery shopping, I received a text message from one of the adult ladies at Bible Club. It included a picture of her, Amy, and Holly posing near the pavilion. Seeing that picture assured me that Amy and Holly were still happily attending Bible Club.

The summer of the following year, I visited Florida on a vacation with my mother. Rachel and her friends invited me to lunch at a restaurant that Sunday afternoon. After I had asked her about Amy and Holly, she informed me that they'd moved out of state less than a month after I had left.

"*Divine appointments—will you see them when they come . . . and, when they come . . . will you be ready to take them on?*"—Those words echoed in my mind that moment.

CHAPTER 48

Reflections

I s there such a thing as a "divine appointment" or is that just a term some preacher made up to describe his gospel opportunities? I can only look back in disbelief every time I ponder the paths in my life—how they winded and twisted around, ultimately leading to a girl's encounter with the gospel. Little did I know that, back in 1997, after praying a short prayer to have a "divine appointment," it would be with someone who wouldn't even be born for the next eight years. Not only that, but I'd then have to wait another eight years to meet this person.

The timing of everything seemed as if no human could've planned it. Consider any number of paths that could've prevented Amy from hearing the gospel:

1. Had PCC never introduced the MBA program, I probably would have left in 2004. I never had plans to stay at PCC unless I was pursuing a degree.

2. Had I not been accepted into staff in the IT department at PCC, I would have left Florida in 2006.

3. Had I not been accepted into a doctoral program, I would have left Florida in 2008.

4. Had I finished my doctoral dissertation on time, I would have left Florida in 2010.

5. Had I not moved into an apartment off campus in 2010, I'd have left Florida after my work contract would've ended on August 1 of 2013. That means I would've either been on the road to Colorado or would've arrived in Colorado around the very day that Amy and Holly first attended Bible Club.

6. Had I had enough money to pay for an early release from my apartment lease, I also would have left for Colorado on August 1 of 2013.

7. Had I not gotten the three-month extension to my work contract granted, I could've ended up working another job that required me to work on Saturdays and miss Bible Club those very months that Amy and Holly began attending.

8. Had Amy's and Holly's mother never noticed the park on her way to an errand and never decided to drop them off, I'd never have met Amy.

9. Had Wayne never asked me to teach a Bible lesson during that time, Amy may have never grasped the gospel.

10. Had I been unwilling to teach another Bible lesson despite my failures, Amy may have never heard it and accepted the gospel.

11. Had I chosen a different date to teach my Bible lesson, it could have been on a day when Amy and Holly were out of town. It could also have been a lesson that I couldn't have used to grab her attention.

12. Had Wayne not cancelled Bible Club on my original Bible lesson date, I wouldn't have been prepared to teach my Bible lesson.

13. Had I not had a dream the following Wednesday night about Amy accepting the gospel, I wouldn't have turned my lesson into an evangelism opportunity.

14. Had Amy not instantly bonded with me when she first met me, she may not have paid as much attention to my Bible lesson. Remember my quiz for the candy? Who wanted candy and who actually wanted to talk to me instead?

15. Had Wayne not asked me to join a group for a restroom break at Home Depot, Amy may not have talked to Rachel about the gospel.

16. Had Amy and Holly moved out of state more than two months prior to when they did, Amy would've never heard my Bible lesson and received the gospel from Rachel.

Had even *one* of *any* of these or other unmentioned paths been even slightly different, Amy may have never accepted the gospel. It boggles the mind how all of these paths connected— most of them based on my petty agendas of pride, greed, laziness, insecurity, and stubbornness.

What should we make of the term "divine appointment?" If such a concept is true, does it only apply to certain scenarios? Could all positive encounters with the gospel be considered "divine appointments?" Could any sincere sharing of the gospel be a "divine appointment?"

Paul wrote in 1 Cor 12:3:

> Wherefore I give you to understand, that no man speaketh by the Spirit of God calleth Jesus accursed: and that no man can say that Jesus is the Lord, but by the Holy Ghost.

If it's a miracle of the Holy Ghost to allow one to call Jesus "Lord" then it could also be the miracle of the Holy Ghost to direct the paths that lead one to the gospel. Even if your gospel experience was more like mine—grew up in a Christian home and believed in Jesus at an early age—how could you determine if your salvation wasn't also the result of a "divine appointment?" The paths the gospel has traveled from Jesus' original apostles at the Great Commission leading up to you may have consisted of more "divine appointments" than anything you or I had ever experienced in our

lives. A ten-thousand-pieced jigsaw puzzle is still amazing when finished even if we only see the first or last few pieces get placed into it.

Now, if you recall the first few chapters of this book, I discussed several witnessing opportunities in which I had engaged—all of them seemed like failures. Why did I even bother including them in this book? Was is because I like to type words? Was I looking for filler in this book to reach a certain word count or chapter count? Was I trying to downplay evangelistic cold callings at people's houses while elevating coincidental "divine appointments?"

My reason for including my "failed" attempts at gospel cold callings (besides adding interesting stories to this book) was to conclude with a thought experiment on the meaning of "divine appointments." Not everyone has to see any path in its entirety to be a valuable part of it. Perhaps, in any of those scenarios, I functioned as just one catalyst along the way that brought someone on a journey to accept the gospel later.

So, what of our original question (and this book's title)? Does God really answer our prayers? Although I've heard the mantras and the Scripture verses about it, I have no mathematical formula to give to you that could explain how anything works. The best I could do is to give you my story and let you make of it however you want. Keep praying and stand in awe of the amazing God we serve!